Jungle Fighter

JUNGLE FIGHTER

Infantry Officer, Chindit & S.O.E. Agent in
Burma, 1941-1945

Major John Hedley, DSO

Tom Donovan
Brighton

First published in 1996 by

Tom Donovan Publishing Ltd.
2 Newport Street
Brighton
East Sussex BN2 3HL

ISBN: 1-871085-34-9

© 1996

Desk-top typeset by Tom Donovan Publishing Ltd.

Printed by Antony Rowe Ltd.

Contents

Maps

Introduction

John Hedley's war memoirs came to light at an antiquarian bookfair in London in 1994 and were brought to the attention of the publisher shortly afterwards. They revealed a wide range of experiences of the war in the Far East: the infantryman's six-month slog through the 1942 retreat; service with the second Chindit expedition, when the author was wounded and mentioned in despatches as Brigade Intelligence Officer to the formidable team of Joe Lentaigne and John Masters; behind-the-lines covert operations with Force 136 and, last but not least, some months in Siam after the war had ended, which provide a valuable personal view of that nation. At that time Hedley came into close contact with the Japanese army and his views on the Japanese character make interesting reading.

For some years before the war J.D.H.Hedley had been employed by the Bombay Burmah Trading Corporation, so he knew the country well. (Field Marshal Slim in his memoirs stated that "...as a class our best intelligence officers were not the government officials, but the outside up-country members of the business firms who had a closer knowledge of the country and its people."). He offered his services on the outbreak of war and on November 13th 1939 went to the first OCTU course run at Maymyo, being gazetted a second lieutenant from that date. The course finished on February 8th 1940; Hedley passed out top and was posted to the 4th Burma Rifles at Kangyi. From July to October 1940 he undertook the Infantry Signals course at Poona - again he passed out top - and returned to the battalion at Mandalay becoming Signals Officer and OC HQ Company. Early in 1941 he did a 3" mortar course at Maymyo and became Mortar officer in May and then Adjutant in July 1941. At the end of October 1941 the battalion moved out to the eastern frontier at Kawkareik, where the main Japanese thrust fell when the war began and they were driven from their positions. Hedley remained with them until sent as interpreter to 63 Brigade, a new brigade from India which had just landed, in March 1942. The same month he became staff captain of the brigade and subsequently Brigade Intelligence Officer. In June 1943 he went to 111 Brigade as Intelligence Officer and trained with them until they flew into the second Chindit expedition in March 1944. In May 1944 he was wounded and on his recovery was posted to Force 136 and promoted to major. He spent the rest of 1944 training and on January 22nd 1945 parachuted into Burma commanding a party which operated behind Japanese lines in the Maymyo area until 25th March. For this operation he was awarded the DSO. In May he parachuted down at Elephant Point, the almost bloodless airborne landing that was part of the advance on Rangoon. After hostilities ended he went with 207 British Military Mission to Siam and was in Siam until he sailed for England in February 1946 for demobilisation.

Hedley is matter-of-fact in describing his own achievements and it is from accounts written by others who knew him, among them John Masters and Richard Rhodes James, that his character is revealed.

He emerges as a highly intelligent and highly regarded officer, who rapidly grasped opportunities and thirsted for knowledge, happiest when there was a difficult task to be undertaken or a new challenge. He appears to have succeeded at everything he attempted and must have been a strong-willed character. His physical powers were legendary and he always walked further and faster than anyone else, often carrying other mens' weapons or kit in addition to his personal armoury. Comments on his personality and achievements will be found in the text where appropriate.

He wrote his 'War History' longhand, and at great speed, on board ship in 1946, probably when he was returning to Burma after a short break at home for demobilisation. While he clearly viewed his experiences as of potential interest to others, he explains that "I wrote it primarily for myself... I started out with the idea of making this a sort of diary with observations and it is my intention to keep it as such. It is not a book, nor was it written as such. If it ever does become one, it will have to be re-written from the start, much more slowly than I have been able to do. Anyone who wishes to is welcome to read it - and if I have been able to impart any of the humour of some of the situations in which I found myself at times in the war, I shall feel my labours well rewarded." The memoirs are published here as they were written, with the minimum of editing.

Sadly, J.D.H.Hedley died in 1979 of a sudden heart attack so did not live to see publication of his 'non-book.' Indeed, the existence of the manuscript came as a surprise to post-war friends and colleagues at Bromsgrove School in Worcestershire where he found his post-war calling as a master, becoming a housemaster and ultimately second master.

Attempts to locate John Hedley's heirs or successors have been unsuccessful, despite contact being made with several people who knew him up to the time of his death. If any of his family read this they are urged to make contact with the publisher.

The publisher's thanks are due to Basil Whitehorn for kindly contributing his own memories of John Hedley.

John Hedley

With great pleasure, but with some hesitancy, I write a few words that will fit properly, I trust with John Hedley's memoirs. I say hesitancy, because it will not be easy to do justice to the unusual person that was John. In some ways he came from an age when people could be called 'encyclopaedic,' so varied and extensive were his qualities. And if I sound rather like the platoon officer who in recommending his sergeant for a medal for valour said, 'He went everywhere I went,' it is because John and I were, in many ways, much connected in the last fifteen years of his life.

I first met him in 1964 when I joined the staff of Bromsgrove School, where John was senior housemaster, and later second master. He was quick to remind me that we had both worked for the same London managing agents, he in Burma with the Bombay Burmah Company, and I in India with the Bombay Company. That remained an unspoken link between us. So too did the fact that we had both served in the war, John in the 14th Army in Burma and I in the Guards Armoured Division in Europe.

Both of us must have been easily 'touched' by anything military, for we spent many happy hours together in the Cadet Force, where John was the training officer. A weekly parade was lightly tolerated, and then there was the promise of an entertaining termly Field Day; the highlight was the summer Camp, when John could let loose his fertile imagination in conjuring up the most impossible schemes. But, as well as that, in company with my children, we tramped over many a Worcestershire site planning events for the cadets, Bredon being our favourite.

He had a fund of regular declamations, eagerly copied by the troops, such as, 'Bring out the dancing girls and let there be high wassail,' or, 'Great howling gorillas,' disastrously translated into French by himself and the 'scholars,' as he used to call them. But as much as any, I enjoyed his oft-repeated phrase, 'my girl-friends,' of which he had two main ones; one small child in London, and the other my youngest daughter, then a few months old. However, this was no special treatment, for every Christmas he went round all the staff children, offering greetings and presents - so typical of his thoughtful and open generosity.

Often on a Sunday afternoon my family and I went for a walk along the canal ending up unannounced at his house, where a welcome and copious tea were assured. He, and his wife Frances, were a couple who certainly knew the meaning of the word hospitality. He was a good family man, and at each camp he would quickly look for a telephone and announce nightly that he was going to 'blow the memsahib.'

When I left the cadets I became co-ordinator of the school Pathfinders, a longstanding activity where boys and girls visited old people at home or in hospital, or wherever there was need among the elderly. John was always keen to provide a 'taxi' for the young; he would then do his own visiting of special friends. He would read to them and comfort them as necessary.

John had a boundless energy. He often told us he wanted to die in harness. His wish was granted for he had a sudden heart attack; shortly after another in hospital that took him home to his Lord. He was not the man to linger on incapacitated. He was then 71.

All his qualities may describe an admirable character, loved by those who knew him well. And a sometimes gruff exterior did not hide his concern for all he met. There was one driving force creating these qualities. He was a regular attender of the daily service in the chapel, and he sang with great gusto, especially his favourite hymn, John Bunyan's pilgrim song, well describing his own character.

> He who would valiant be
> 'gainst all disaster
> let him in constancy
> follow the master
> there's no discouragement
> shall make him once relent
> his first avowed intent
> to be a pilgrim.

In one word, it was his Faith.

Basil Whitehorn
June 1996

1

The Retreat from Burma

The war, as far as I was concerned, began on 13th November, 1939, when I was sent on the first OCTU at Maymyo. There were about 36 of us in all, and the Bombay Burmah Trading Corporation Ltd. (BBTCL) was well represented as, in addition to myself, there were Shelley Griffiths, Herring, R.W. Wood, Macpherson, E.W. Booker, Buchanan and Gates for certain, and may have been more. I don't think there is much doubt that the first was the best course to be on. They made us officers from the start, which was very pleasant, and we had the advantage, in my opinion, of being in Maymyo for the cold weather.

We were all lodged in Craddock Court, two blocks of flats being for us, one block for married students, and one being for officers and instructors. Messing was communal in the dining hall in the centre of the compound. I shared a flat with E.W. Booker.

The course lasted until 8th February, and I've seldom spent a pleasanter time. A grand lot of blokes, cheerful and enthusiastic instructors, good weather, plenty of games, and interesting work. The course, for me, had one further advantage, namely that it was during it I first met my wife. So generally things could hardly have been pleasanter. The war seemed an almost infinite distance away, and even when you got to it, was still only the "phoney" war at that time. It was, therefore, not very easy to work up tremendous martial ardour, nor that attitude of "suspicious alertness" which we were afterwards told was so necessary: for we thought, with good reason then, that the most any of us would ever see of war would be guard duties in Maymyo and Mandalay. Nearly all of us, and certainly myself, applied to go home when we passed out, but we were told, as expected, that it was quite out of the question. A sense of disappointment was not unnatural.

In the circumstances, it would not have been surprising had people taken the course somewhat casually, but very few did, and, as subsequent war history has proved, the standard of officer turned out was extremely high.

The instructors, as stated, were cheerful and enthusiastic, and in my opinion gave us a thoroughly sound grounding. It is useless to try and maintain that our tactics were not somewhat out of date. The first two years of the war in Europe and Asia alike proved that the tactics of the entire Imperial Armies were years behind those of the enemy; so why should Burma be blamed more than any other? The CO was Lt.-Col. Fletcher, who was an excellent man for the job, as he was a man of infectious enthusiasm, and I liked him very much. My squad instructor was Capt. Appleby, of the 3rd Burma Rifles, and I liked him too. The work was interesting and not unduly exacting - by my standards, anyway. I took part in all games, but my prime object was to pass out top, and this I managed to do fairly easily in the exams in February 1940.

I knew sometime previously that I was going to 4th Burma Rifles: So, when a very pleasant course ended, to them I went.

4th Burma Rifles

The Battalion, under Lt.-Col. H. Dawes, was in camp at Kangyi, some miles from Maymyo, and I joined them there. There were two or three other battalions there. There was less than a month of camp left to run when we arrived so we only saw the end of it. The time there was enjoyable and interesting, but even at the time the form of training seemed out of place, and looking back on it now (1946) one can see how hopelessly wrong our training and tactics were. As already stated, it's no use blaming Burma when the whole Imperial Armies were at fault, but it doesn't alter the fact that we WERE wrong. Here we were in the middle of Burma, a country covered largely in jungle. One would therefore, have thought that most of the training would have been done in the jungle: Not a bit of it, Kangyi was apparently selected as being the closest approximation to Salisbury plain which could be found, and our training was modelled almost exactly on the lines of Salisbury plain for the Western Desert, without of course having the necessary tank and artillery support - even in theory. Some of the training, of course, was of value in being a constant in all forms of warfare - toughening, march discipline, administration etc. and one or two specialised forms of tactics, such as internal security, but the general tactical training was no use for fighting in Burma, as we were to be shown by the Japanese in due course. The effects of this type of training were, in my opinion particularly disastrous in the case of the Burma Rifles. The Burma riflemen, we had only Kachins, Karens and Chlis in my battalion - is a hillman and a jungleman. From time immemorial he has been used to fighting by the methods best adapted to the hill and the jungle-mobility, ambush, quick attack and withdrawal, hitting where least expected, and never staying in one place for long. These principles of jungle warfare are as correct for an army as for a band of dacoits or villagers, and the Japanese were far sighted enough to model their

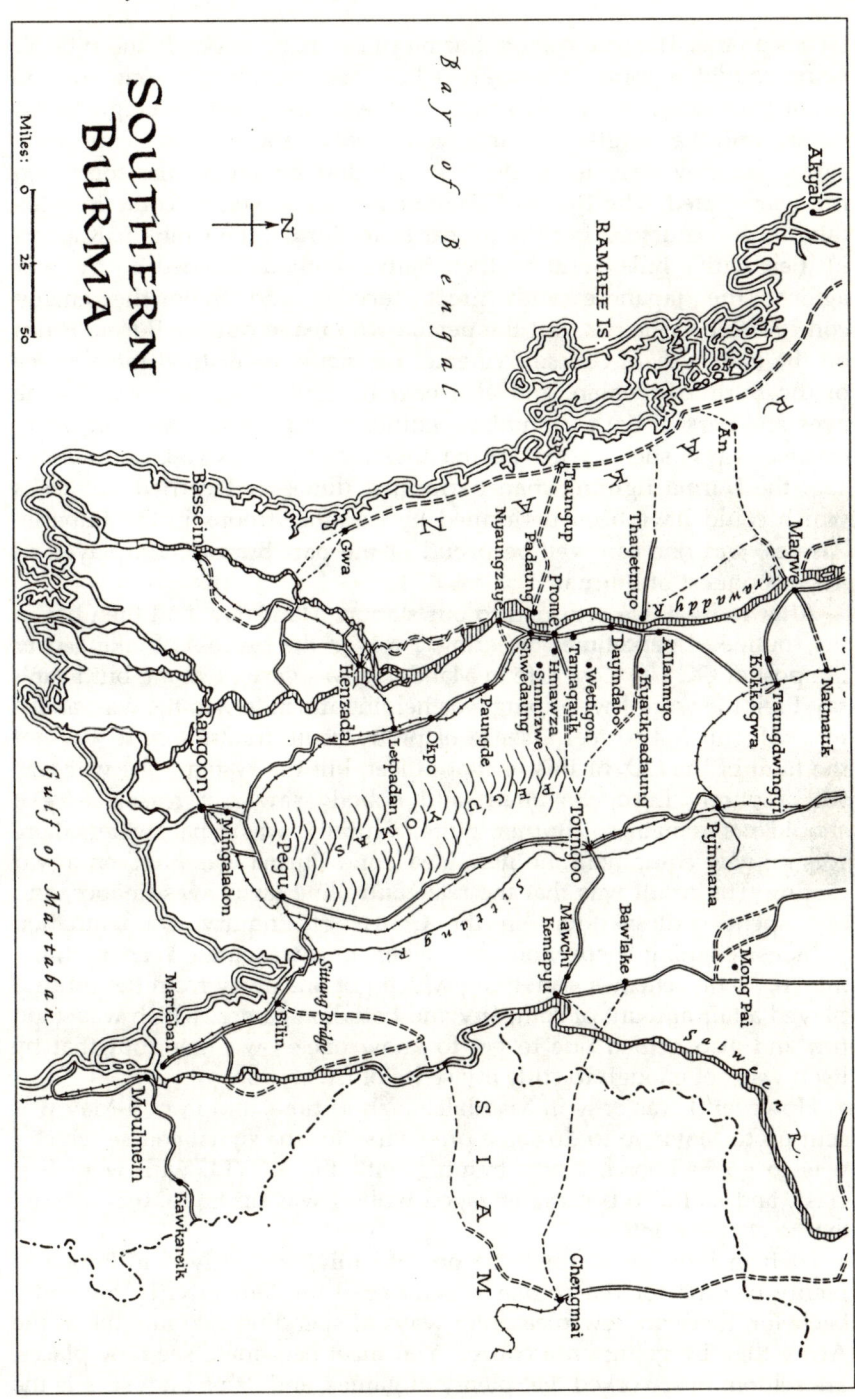

SOUTHERN BURMA

Miles: 0 25 50

N

Bay of Bengal

RAMREE IS.

Gulf of Martaban

Bassein
Gwa
Rangoon
Henzada
Okpo
Leipadan
Pegu
Mingaladon
Martaban
Bilin
Sittang Bridge
Moulmein
Kawkareik

Paungde
Nyaungzaya
Padaung
Prome
Taungup
Shwedaung
Sinmizwe
Hmawza
Tamagauk
Wetigon
Dayindabo
Kyaukpadaung
Allanmyo
Thayetmyo
An
Magwe
Natmauk
Taungdwingyi
Kokkogwa
Pyinmana
Toungoo
Mawchi
Kemapyu
Bawlake
Mong Pai
Chengmai

Irrawaddy R.
Salween R.
Sittang R.

A R A K A N

P E G U Y O M A S

S I A M

tactics on the. The unfortunate Burma rifleman, however, found himself being taught a form of warfare which was not only wrong for the country in which he was to fight, but was also totally foreign to his nature; and the results, of course were what one would have expected - as indeed they were for units of British and Indian Armies too when the war started. The Burma Rifleman was, however, to come into his own in due course. After the retreat from Burma, the Chins & Kachins in their native hills - and by their native methods, carried on the war against the Japanese with great success, and gave the enemy considerable casualties. But the person who really put the Burma Rifles on the map was, of course, Wingate. He really understood the abilities of the Burma Rifleman, and also how he could best be used. As the eyes and ears of both Chindit expeditions, and subsequently in many diverse ways- such as the Burma Intelligence Corps (BIC) and Force 136, the Burma fighting man performed duties and carried out tasks which could have been performed by no other troops in the Imperial Armies, and one can well be proud of the part Burma men played in the reconquest of Burma.

After Kangyi, we returned to our station, Mandalay, and then began the routine of peacetime soldiering. I was in the process of taking over the post of OC HQ Coy. Life in Mandalay was very pleasant, but I can't say I felt the work I was doing was helping much to win the war, and it was difficult not to feel a sense of pretty acute frustration. It was not the fault of the CO, or this or that officer, but the system. The war was still a purely European affair, and nobody saw any reason why it should not remain so; Burma, quite naturally, was a backwater, there was no new equipment, no new ideas, and Burma was NOT on a war footing. The result was that the real controlling factor was finance, and one spent endless hours in the Courts of Enquiry, condemnation parades, clothing inspections etc. when one was mad keen to train, march, go on schemes - anything which got one away from the office. I played a fair amount of company and battalion games, which was good fun and also helped one to get to know one's own men, but that by itself was not enough to stifle my sense of frustration.

However, I was only in Mandalay a short time, and in mid-May was sent up to Maymyo to do some pre-course for the signal course which I was to go in Poona, I was training with the KOYLI, who were first class, and as I also became engaged while I was up there, time passed extremely pleasantly.

I left in July, sailed for India on 15th July, and arrived in Poona in plenty of time for the course which began on 28th July. If you are a bachelor, there are few pleasanter ways of spending two months in the Army than by going on a course. You meet new men, see new places, are seldom overworked, get plenty of games, and - this I am sure is the chief reason why men like a course so much - have no responsibility apart from passing the course. I found signalling great fun, and, with the initial advantage of having been trained by Sgt. Dolman of the KOYLI, passed top and got a "special." I was asked to go back as an instructor, but my battalion would not hear of it. I returned to Burma in October, was married in November, and settled down to - as we thought - indefinite regimental soldiering in Mandalay. At that time I was OC HQ Coy. and, of course, Signals Officer. The work was much more interesting by reason of having a signals platoon to train, but even so one was terribly clogged by paper work. However life was very pleasant. It was not however to continue so for long, as early in March the whole battalion was ordered down to Moulmein, and, as Moulmein was not a family station, my wife had to stay in Maymyo.

Moulmein

We arrived in Moulmein on 5th March, and as our semi-permanent camp had not been built, we camped for the first month or two at Rookmanund's bathing pool, some three miles out of Moulmein to the south. The battalion was by this time under the command of Lt.-Col. P.P. Abernethy, whose ideas on training, in my opinion, were considerably ahead of most other officers, and of whom I was very fond. There was still a goodly amount of coggage to be ploughed through, but there were far better facilities for doing some training too. By this time, however, a new snag had arisen - inevitable but none the less a snag - equipment. As was natural, Burma was still a very low priority and much of our equipment was very old, and not much new stuff was forthcoming. However, we did the best we could, and certainly it was a great improvement on Mandalay life, as far as becoming an efficient soldier was concerned.

I had one or two interludes. In May I was sent to Maymyo for a 3" Mortar course, and also got ten days leave in Maymyo a bit later. On return, therefore, I was OC HQ Coy., Signals Officer, and as in July our adjutant went on a staff job, I became Adjutant also. By this time, however, I had given up OC HQ Coy. and Mortar Officer, but even so had a hard days work. In May we moved into our semi-permanent camp, which was at Mile 6 south of Moulmein, and was very comfortable. In June I took my signal platoon out to Kawkabeth to report on the position from a signals point of view, but apart from that and the fact that we had 275 inches of rain that monsoon, I don't think there's much else to report about Moulmein. By the Monsoon we had the 2nd Burma Rifles and a mountain battery with us, and Moulmein was a brigade HQ. So passed the rains of 1941.

Kawkareik

Towards the end of October the battalion left Moulmein for Kawkareik, ostensibly for training, but we were never to see that camp again. There were only two ways to Kawkareik by which, at any rate, supplies could be sent up - one by water, which in any case only went as far as Kyondo, after which there was a 13 mile stretch of road to Kawkareik. The other was by road all the way. The road went very far south, was largely through jungle, and had about 40 wooden rickety bridges on it, at many of which even the 30 cwt lorries which we had had to be unloaded; furthermore, there were two river crossings, at each of which there was a single ferry, capable of taking one lorry only. So the L of C was as tenuous as could reasonably be imagined. During the previous rains it had been examined by the sappers, but nothing had been done about it, partly I suppose owing to the lack of the necessary personnel and materials, but chiefly because the general staff always thought that the main attack when it came would be through the Shan States and not Tenasserim.

We arrived in two days, by road, and stayed a day or two at Kawkareik. Its a pretty part of the world. Kawkareik is at the foot of the Dawnas, which rises very sharply to about 2600-3500 feet, and are covered in a very stiff jungle. The road runs north for about ten miles along the bottom of the hills, and then zigzags up over the top, a really stiff climb for MT. There are one or two sheer cliffs on the road - ideal places for demolitions. The road then runs roughly along the top of the pass for some six miles, to Sukli rest house, and from there you get a glorious view of the plain beyond, over the Thoungyin river, which is the Siamese frontier, and thence to the hills in Siam beyond. To anyone wanting a peaceful time, it would be hard to imagine a better setting, but we were there to dig defences.

That was what we did for the next few weeks - that and patrolling up to the Thoungyin, which was some ten miles away by road. Being Adjutant and Signals Officer, I was debarred from going on any of these, unfortunately. We were in comfortable tents, the weather was perfect, and supplies arrived regularly through Moulmein; and you can believe it or not, but they regularly sent us up FIREWOOD: such is the red tape. We had various visits, including one from Major-Gen. Smyth VC who had taken over the division, and from Lt.-Gen. Hutton, who had then taken over Burma command. Things by, say mid-November, were clearly blowing up somewhat, and we had a regular detachment of sappers to prepare demolitions on the road. Japan had declared war. I can well remember the stunned gloom which descended on the mess when we heard over the wireless about the sinking of the *Prince of Wales* and *Repulse*.

Japanese forces having overrun Siam, it was clear that it wouldn't be long before we had Japanese troops watching us from across the Thoungyin, and soon Siam was to come in against us too. The defence of the area was hampered by reason of the fact that some of troops had to be maintained at Myawadi, on the Thoungyin, as this was the very furthest point east and so could give first warning by telephone of Japanese aircraft going to raid Rangoon. We saw several flights of them going over. The company there was, of course, hopelessly isolated. Far better, but for Myawadi, it would have been to hold the hills on the road and the few paths over them, and just patrol forward to the river.

For the whole of December and early part of January we were the only battalion there, and such war as there was was of a somewhat comic nature. One occasionally got a shot at a bloke the other side of the river who might have been a Jap or Siamese, but the chief 'action' centred round the Myawadi rice mill. This was in operation as usual, but the Siamese the other side thought that it would be a grand joke to fire a few shots through the building whenever work began. Not unnaturally this caused the mill to stop work, and this happened three or four days running: until, happy thought, the millers appealed to the 4th Burma Rifles. So the following day we prepared an ambush, and when the mill opened up and the Siamese tried their tricks, we rubbed out about 20 with Mortar and LMG fire and thereafter the mill was able to work unmolested.

About the middle of January they made Kawkareik a brigade, the 1/9th Jats and the 1/7th Gurkhas being sent up to reinforce us, and we were put under a new Brigadier and Brigade staff. Moulmein was under our old Brigadier, Bourke by name. The new Brigadier decided to pull us back into reserve, in the Kawkareik area, and to bring up the new battalions onto the hill. He was also going to change over units of these battalions with units of ours which were blocking the small tracks north and south of the main road. Actually, the change-over was about half completed when the Japanese struck and the number of separate units dotted about the countryside ran to about ten. Suffice it here to say that the most of the 1/7th Gurkhas were on the hill, most of the Jats were still in the Kawkareik, one company of the Jats was east of the hills guarding the track to the south, and the Burma Rifles were spread all over the place.

I have said, and I have heard said, more bitter things about the so-called battle (?) of Kawkareik than any other subject in the course of the war. Certainly when I got back to Moulmein I told Brig. Bourke and his staff what I thought of Kawkareik and its Brigadier in terms - mostly beginning with the consonant 'b' - for which I could have been put under arrest on the spot. But by then I was so fighting mad I didn't care about anything. As, however, at this distance in time, there is nothing to be gained by standing once more in condemnation of the incident, I shall do what I can to whitewash it.

Now I'm NOT, repeat NOT, going to go to the extent of saying I think the Brigadier did right, which I do NOT, but I will admit that there were extenuations. One was the fact that the Japs had by then got Tavoy: so sooner or later would be able to cut our lines of communication. A second was that the Jats had 50% recruits and as a result were not reliable - no real fault of theirs. The last, however, and by far the greatest, was the old story: the Japs were trained to jungle fighting: we were not. Everything they did was a surprise, and it was this sense of doubt and confusion in the Brigadier's mind, I'm sure, which produced his hasty and ill-conceived plan. And, mark you, this was only the first time. The Japanese tactics of encirclement through the jungle were destined to bring about - during the campaign - one bloodless withdrawal after another: and it was that fact; their tactics being right and ours wrong, which would have lost us the Burma campaign no matter what aircraft we had. The bravest men are useless in battle if wrongly trained. Another extenuation which I should have mentioned is that the lines of communication were soon rendered useless for lorries by bombing of the ferries, as everyone knew they would be.

Now for the battle. I have made a sketch map which makes no pretence of being to scale, and only shows the salient features. When the Japanese struck there was a company of the 1/7th GR at Myawadi, a company of the 1/9th Jats on the track to the south - the rest of the Jats were at Kawkareik - and the 4th BR and 1/7th GR were divided between the main positions in the Sukli area, Kawkareik and the track to the North. Kyondo was our dump, and had been and was being stocked by river, and from Kyondo the supplies were lorried up to the troops. The road through Kya-In was the road to Moulmein, and at Kya-In there was one of the two ferries.

As can be seen, all the Japanese had to do was to bomb Kya-In and Kyondo and our L of C became pretty well hopeless. This they did and it did. They got a direct hit on the Kya-In ferry, and that was the end of any chance of getting lorries across there. They then hit the unloading jetty at Kyondo and, although that would not have been an insuperable objection, their air superiority would in a short time have made it impossible for us to get river steamers up with supplies. So the supply position was soon hopeless. However, we had quite large supplies at

Kyondo, and could have held out for some time as far as food etc. was concerned.

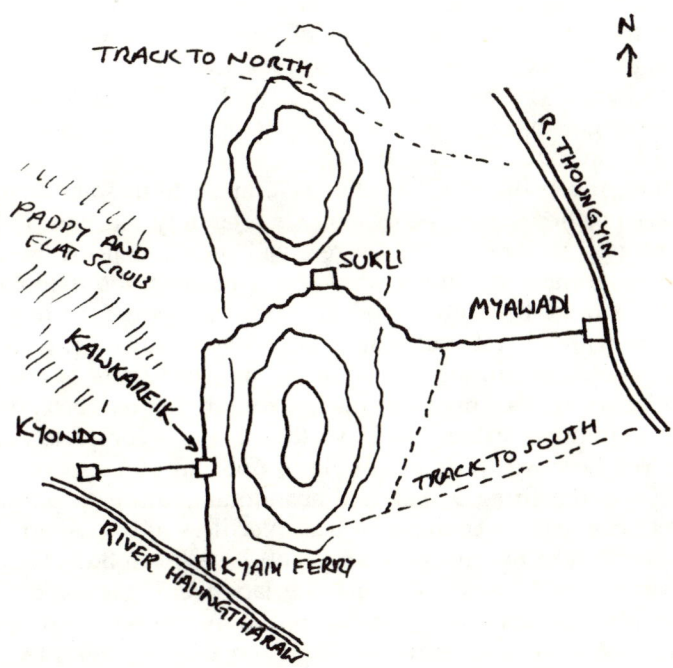

The Japanese attacked at dawn on 20th January 1942. They surrounded the Company at Myawadi, as it was also obvious that they would, but the Company fought its way out and got back to the main positions in the Sukli area. Simultaneously they attacked and dispersed the company of the 1/9th Jats on the southern track. Lt.-Col. White of the 1/7th GR went forward to see what had happened, and was ambushed. He was reported missing but subsequently turned up. Unfortunately, however, Raymond Hall was killed in this ambush. He had been Steels' forest representative in this area, and had been taken on as an intelligence officer. He was absolutely invaluable, as he not only knew the area backwards, but also was greatly beloved and respected by the villagers. He was a fine man and his death in action was a great blow.

Lt.-Col. White having been reported missing, my colonel, Lt.-Col. Abernethy was ordered up to Sukli to take over the forward positions, and as his Adjutant I went with him.

So passed the night of 20th/21st January. Up to this time there had been some bombing of the main positions, but no attacks of any sort.

On the 21st Lt.-Col. White turned up once more: so Abernethy and self went back to the Kawkareik area - actually we were about five miles north of Kawkareik. The position then was that there had been no attack on the main position, but the narrow 12 miles track leading through the hills and coming up south of Kawkareik was in the hands of the Japs. On the other hand, this track was very difficult, and had been blocked by us - so far as possible, and I don't suppose even mules could have got through. there didn't, therefore, really seem to be any reason for particular alarm.

Nothing much happened on the 21st, apart from some bombing of the Sukli positions, and then came 22nd January - a date I shall not easily forget. At about noon we received orders that on the night of 22nd/23rd January all stores would be destroyed, the demolitions on the road would be blown, and the brigade would march back to Moulmein with what it could carry! I don't ever remember feeling more utterly bewildered during the whole of my life. There is one type of defence only - the last man and the last round; that had been drummed into us in training at the OCTU, so that it was a completely accepted axiom. Yet, here we were, proposing to pull out of a superb defensive position without firing a shot, and abandoning all our equipment. We couldn't believe it - it couldn't be true. Needless to say, Abernethy was not a man to take that lying down, so off he went to Bde HQ, and was told that the right flank was gone, the Japs were "getting round us" - how often we were to hear that during the Burma war, and usually on utterly flimsy or non-existent evidence, and that as the L of C was cut for all MT - which was true, we had not option.

Abernethy argued for all he was worth, but to no avail, and at about 2100 hours on 22nd January the retreat was due to start. I don't ever remember spending a glummer day - a day spent in reflecting that after one-and-a-half years of really hard work with one's battalion, and we *had* worked hard in that time - the whole thing was going to be thrown to the winds at 9 o'clock that night. I've had some bad moments in this was, but I still look back to that as the worst of all. Helpless frustration and a feeling of profound humiliation were my chief sentiments, and they are not pleasant when combined. Abernethy was as fighting mad as ever I've seen him, and finally decided that whatever orders he had received, he was going to try and get our mules and equipment back to Moulmein. So passed that cheerless day.

The plan, so far as there can be said to have been one, was that starting at 2100 hours and ending at midnight the troops from the Sukli positions would come down by lorry, and go through Kawkareik to Kyondo. We would withdraw through Kawkareik in the early morning of the 23rd, and the troops in Kawkareik would be the last of all to withdraw.

The troops from the hill came down all right, and I can still remember the thunderous roar - although it was ten miles away, as at midnight the road along the face of the Kyaukaba Taung disappeared over a 700-foot cliff; a perfect spot for a demolition. We started at about 2 am, and as the mules would be slower than we who were in lorries, the mules were sent ahead. We followed at about 0400 hours, to catch them up about half a mile north of Kawkareik, not as might be expected going towards Kawkareik, but coming out of it as fast as the mules could gallop, having been shot up on approaching the village. Helter skelter they went up the road, into the jungle, anywhere. It was heartbreaking but by then it was useless trying to chase them. We soon found out that the people who shot us up were the Jats - this happened over and over again in Burma - and in other theatres too for that matter - but the CO had to assume that it was the Japs who were in Kawkareik, so we had to abandon our mules, and, without going through Kawkareik, began our march back to Moulmein. The Japs were not, I know, in Kawkareik until the following afternoon, as at eight o'clock that morning one of our men walked through Kawkareik, and at 11.15 we saw the Japs bombing the lorries which we had left two miles north of the village. The Jats reported large numbers of Japs - at NIGHT, of course, in the paddy south of Kawkareik, and fired a good many thousands of rounds at these nebulous samurai. It is possibly this fact which produced the illuminating BBC broadcast to the effect that:

> Our troops, after carrying out the prearranged demolition programme, have withdrawn from positions in the Kawkareik area in good order. Hundreds of the enemy were mown down by our fire.

The final insult. Operation "Italian Waiter" was over. Sick at heart we marched back to Moulmein.

Kawkareik was the result of people losing their heads when flustered by utterly new tactics employed by a new enemy, and the situation was further aggravated by certainly exaggerated, and possibly quite untrue, reports of enemy encirclement from the right flank.

What should have been done? In the various extenuating circumstances I have already said that in my opinion the position would have had to have been abandoned sooner or later, and with the ferries gone and the air against us we could never have got the lorries back, but I am convinced we should never have legged it the way we did. Clearly what we should have done was

1. Held Sukli positions.

2. Kept strong flank guards to the right: if necessary withdrawing some troops from Sukli.

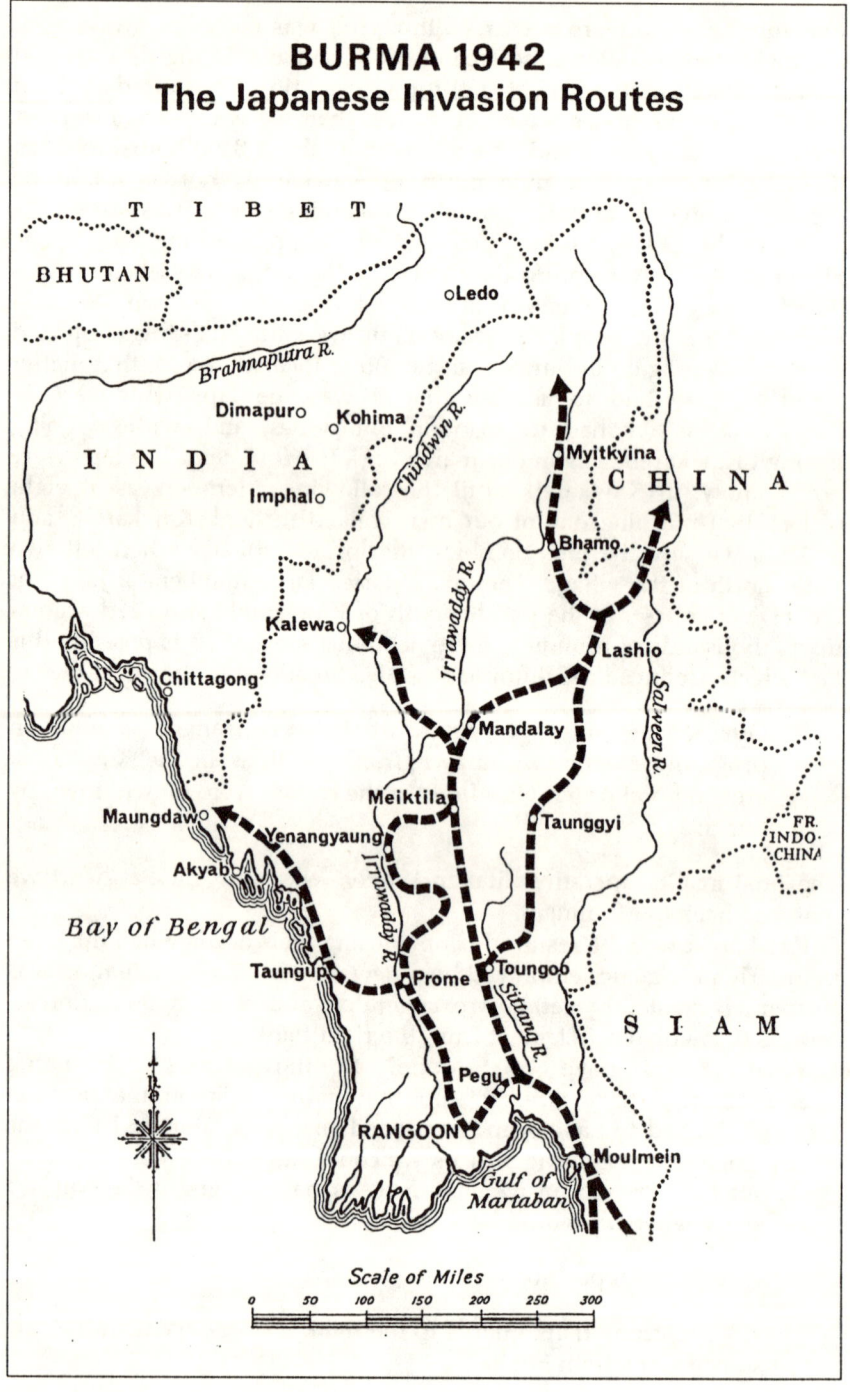

BURMA 1942
The Japanese Invasion Routes

3. Commandeered everything which would float: sampans, rafts, anything, and on these get our weapons down to Moulmein.

4. March the men and mules back when the more important stores had been got away, and swim the mules across the rivers.

Had we done this we would have arrived a fighting brigade in Moulmein - and with our morale high - and one brigade might have made the defence of Moulmein possible and given vital time further back. As it was, we were 2500 men armed with rifles, and on arrival were sent straight over to Martaban and thence further west.

So ended my first battle (??). The effect on British officers was bad enough, and the effect on the native troops can well be imagined. It was my first real insight into the state of uncertainty one can get into by the confusion of battle, and while I can't agree the commander was right, I can at least sympathise with him. After Kawkareik I was prepared to bet nothing could surprise me - but it did not take long to dispel that juvenile illusion.

Martaban to Sittang

By the time we had all reassembled we were stationed in the village of Kywegan, some 12 miles from Martaban, and not long after that were pushed further back to Thaton. As this is an account, primarily, of my own war experiences, I shall endeavour, as far as possible, to leave out long descriptions of strategic and tactical dispositions, but a certain amount will be necessary from time to time. By now there were considerably larger forces in the Thaton-Martaban area and Moulmein did not fall until 31st January. When it fell, however, the Japanese had freedom to strike anyway they chose up the Salween river, or, for that matter, on the coast west of Martaban. As it turned out, they subsequently did both, landing behind the Martaban position and making it untenable and overwhelming the 7/10th Baluch Regiment at Paan after the bloodiest action of the war. The 7/10th put up a superlative show, lost 500 out of 700, and were only beaten by weight of numbers. It is estimated the Japs had 600 killed out of 2000 - a glorious action.

The result of this uncertainty was that battalions were being split up and companies being sent piecemeal all over the place. At Thaton, therefore, three of our companies were sent to various places. The remainder of us were at the railway station and it was there that, on 4th February, very tired and by the aid of a flickering light, I deciphered a signal one evening and found I was the father of a daughter.

My paternity was, however, nearly cut short, as at 2.30 the following afternoon the familiar sound of Jap aircraft was heard. We wondered whose turn it was this time and it didn't take us long to find out. Of course, we had slit trenches dug, and were well at the bottom of them when the first wave arrived. There were three aircraft in each wave and we must have been as sitting a mark as any bomber could want. No ground or air opposition, perfect visibility, and a dead straight railway line to fly down. The worst part of all was waiting for the second wave. When the first wave came there was just a chance, even then, that we were NOT the objective, but the second wave we KNEW was for us, and so it was. However, it was soon over and though they hit the line and got right in amongst us, nobody was hurt, and I don't remember anyone, in the whole campaign, being killed in a slit trench. It was my first time under fire, and might have been worse. We spent the next hour unloading petrol from a train in the station, as there was a house blazing nearby, and then moved off to Kyet-Too-Ywa-Thaung, a village on the river Donthami, a tributary of the Salween to the north of Thaton.

Meanwhile the Japs were doing their usual trick, encircling with a view to cutting L of C, and further withdrawals took place. We marched back to Bilin, and then railed back to Kyaitko. It was on one of these withdrawals - all of which, of course, were done by night, that one battalion discovered afterwards it had had a battalion of Japanese marching 100 yards behind it, both being oblivious of the identity of the other!

We remained some days at Kyaitko, the only excitement being when the Japs one night sent perhaps two sections to fire red tracer into our positions; at a conservative estimate our troops fired 100,000 rounds in reply, which must have given the Japs some small satisfaction and also a fairly clear indication as to the whereabouts of our troops.

However, it had already been decided we were to withdraw from Kyaitko, as it was known that the Jap 55th Infantry Division was going through the jungle to the north to get to the Sittang river before us. The hurry was such that we were to withdraw from Kyaitko by day. Now west of Kyaitko there is a two-and-a-half mile strip of paddy, without a tree or bit of cover of any sort on it. We were such a sitting target that the army said we must have air cover even if it meant denuding Rangoon of air defence for a day. The RAF agreed, and we then had one of the most poetic examples of what can be done by staff work which the war produced.

The Army Air Liaison Officer was the genius concerned: he told the RAF where we were, and where the Japs were: he gave the RAF a line over which they were not to bomb or machine-gun, and he gave them points which they were expected to pass hour by hour. He only made one mistake - he said we were the Japs and the Japs were us. So the only time we had the RAF in close support they were circling over the Jap 55th Div at 100 feet and waving to them, and roaring down over us in the paddy fields at anything from 150 to 15 feet. Now there's an artistry about staff work of that nature, no question of laboriously working out a map reference wrong - just the insolent ease of a man who knows he can box his job up and what's more how he's going to box it up. We spread out and lay down, of course, and the total bag in our battalion, from five Hurricanes and one Tomahawk was one wounded! But on the road through the paddyfields they did fearful destruction to the transport. The worst thing they did, of course, was to delay us, and many who were caught at Sittang might have got over but for that error - just two words wrong. The RAF were not of course to blame. I had the nearest escape I ever had when a Hurricane came down to about 30 feet. I was lying down behind a bund, too small to stop bullets and too low to cover me, and I'll see that blasted fellow coming at me to my dying day. He was aiming at me, I'll swear he was, and he opened up at 150 yards: I could see the tracer just a few inches over my head, and if he'd pulled the trigger 1/10th of a second earlier this would never have been written - seems tough, doesn't it.

We spent the night in the jungle nearby, and the day after moved off to Sittang. Kyaitko could claim parity with Kawkareik.

Sittang

"As a complete military box up, the Sittang battle was technically perfect."

"The Sittang battle was qualitatively, though not quantitatively, the biggest box up of the war."

These two dicta, both from the pen of a leading military commentator, may be overstatements, but joking apart, I never remember any situation in which one felt so helpless. It wasn't that one was in great danger or anything of that sort, it simply was that the fog of war was of such a concentrated density that nobody knew what was going on, or to start off with what we were expected to do.

We arrived at Mokpalin, from the south at about noon on 21st February and, in all, three brigades, from all directions, were pouring in or had poured in to Sittang and Mokpalin. There were masses of troops but no staffs - brigade staffs that is, and a few hours were spent in trying to find anyone to give orders. More enterprising COs were

taking action on their own, and it is now known that it was in this
confusion that two battalions fought EACH OTHER. We were at the
south of the railway station but west of the line, and throughout the
day the Japs were attacking on the other side of the line, but got no
change out of the 8th Burma Rifles. After a bit the Kawkareik Brigadier
turned up, though he was not our Brigadier, and really did get things
organised. We were very glad to see him. We were to form a box
around Mokpalin, we being on the SW corner.

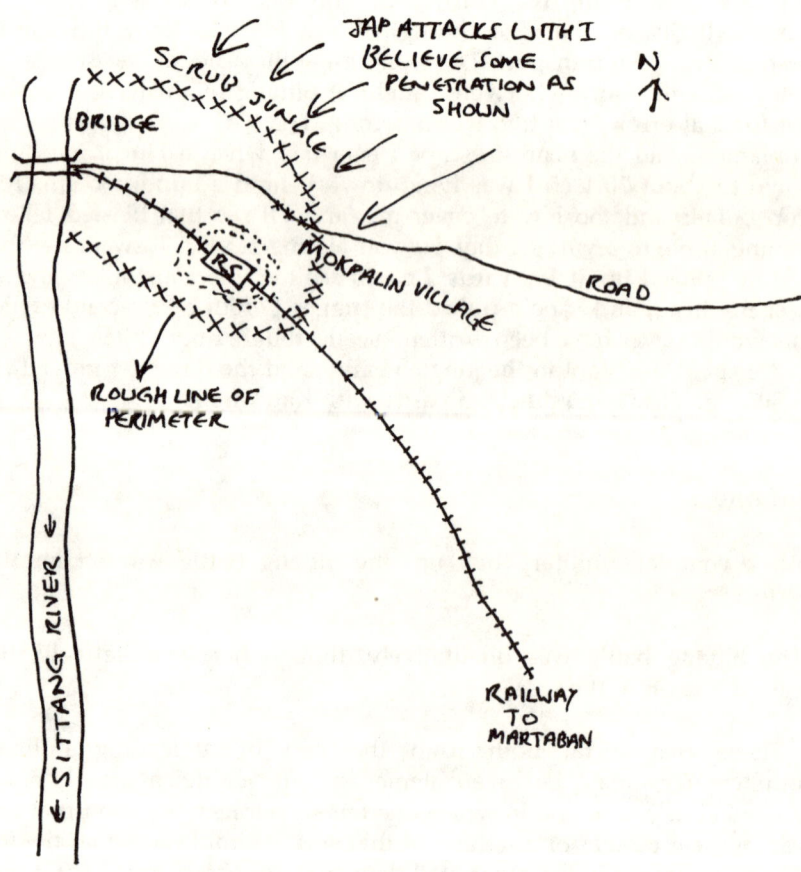

Meanwhile, fighting was going on to the north, and it is NOW clear
what was happening. The Japanese 55th Div had raced to get to the
bridge before us, and failed. They had, however, come from the

north-east. So, as will be seen from the map, only the left fringe of the Jap force would hit us: the main attack, of course, would go in further north. By the evening of the 21st, therefore, some sort of order had been established, largely owing to the Brigadier's efforts, and our own brigade staff had by then turned up. We settled down for the night in Mokpalin village, sleep being interrupted by a series of Jap bombardments. These, however, were not severe and caused few casualties, but at 0500 hrs there was a blinding flash and a colossal roar - the bridge! We all knew it had gone, but everyone made out it was something else! But it was the bridge all right.

So we woke up on the morning of 22nd February to the realisation that we had a river behind us but a bridge with two rather important gaps in it. It had by now, of course, been decided that we should withdraw across the river, and the method was quite correct. A box was to be held, while the troops got across, and the last troops were to get across the following night. We were to hold on until 7.30 pm.

During the day there was some shelling and sniping by the Japs, but the most unpleasant experience was to see a Jap bomber come over and see the blasted bombs all the way down. A great friend and brother officer of mine, Capt. Gemmell was lying beside me, and I thought it was all over. The first was 100 yards short, the second 50, and the third SIX! Luckily the bombs were diggers, and so went in before exploding, otherwise that also might have interfered with the production of this manuscript. By 1 pm there were only about 20 of us left in our particular sector, as a large number of troops had been withdrawn, and not a few, of all sorts, had withdrawn themselves. However, there were no Japanese attacks, partly because I don't think they were interested after they had failed to save the bridge and partly because we were too far to the Jap left. We did, however, have one incident, and I was able to observe one of the most calculatedly brave acts I've ever seen. During the afternoon we saw a Jap patrol at a range of about 500 yards. They were gloriously outlined against a grass bank and, better still, bunched up to have a confabulation about future patrol policy. We had a Kachin jemadar (sergeant) of my battalion who was a fine shot, and with one long burst of a Bren he got the whole lot bar one. Did that man beat it? Did he hell. He nipped up half way up the bank and SAT DOWN! We fired one shot - a foot left, another - a foot right - a burst - all right - another burst - low. Then and then alone did he beat it, and within three minutes we had grenade dischargers firing at us and had to move. He was NOT going to move till he knew where our LMG was, and he was prepared to offer his own body as a sitting target in order to find out.

During the day we had been collecting bamboo from the houses in Mokpalin, and at 7.30 got together and carried it down to the river.

Hugo Hinds, Forest Dept and my battalion, was with us, and with his aid we made a first class raft. We were going to put our equipment on top and swim it across all holding it, and were just ready when down came four wounded. So that was the end of the raft. We put the wounded on, picked five KOYLI and five Burma Riflemen out of our party, and sent them off. I'm glad to say I heard afterwards the wounded had got back. The confusion on the bank at this time was pretty bad. I should think there was anything up to one brigade's arms and equipment on the bank, and the Japs must have had a rich haul from it.

We were then minus any bamboo; so we went back in considerable trepidation - speaking for self at any rate, to get some more. The village was largely burning by then, and might well be 'inhabited,' we thought. However, we needn't have worried, as there was nobody there, and we got our bamboo and returned once more to the charge. We made another raft, got all our stuff on, and were ready to go, when an unfortunate Indian mule driver came up and asked to come with us. Hinds quite correctly said "No" as it might endanger the whole lot, and I was in some perplexity as to what to do, as the mule driver had assured me that by some extraordinary natural phenomenon I was both his father AND mother. Providence, in the form of an almirah solved the question. This came floating past, and so off we started, self, the mule driver and one Burma Rifleman on the almirah and Hinds and the rest on the raft. It took two-and-a-half hours to get over, and, of course, we got parted from my kit and equipment. But we got over in the end. On arrival I met a bloke in the 1/3rd GR who asked me to take a boat back to fetch wounded from the far bank. We managed to make two trips and get about 20 wounded before dawn. At dawn I was on the west bank, and was wondering whether to go back when a volley of shots from the other side and two white flags indicated that the Japs had closed in and the unfortunate survivors were prisoners.

So ended those memorable two days. Controversy at the time, of course was very bitter, but I'd like to meet the man who blew the bridge. He had a ghastly decision to make, and I'd like to tell him that I think he was right, and that by his courage he probably saved us from being in a far worse plight. Had the Japanese got the Sittang bridge complete, they could have gone bald-headed for Rangoon with - then - nothing much to stop them. As it was, they turned north, and much vital time was saved for us. I was almost the last man across, and so can't be accused of being an armchair critic, but I salute the man who made that courageous and ghastly decision.

On finally reaching the west bank, I realised two things, one was that I was really tired, and the other that I had lost my arms and equipment - which had gone on the raft. However, quite soon Gemmell turned up, and was a real good friend to me. The Japs obviously weren't going to cross; so we rested for two hours. It was obviously going to be a hard march for me, as I thought we were going to have to march 35 miles to Pegu, and my boots and socks were with my equipment on the raft. Paddy fields, believe me, are hot and sharp on bare feet by day at the end of February, and I owe a real debt to Gemmell for the help he was. We did 12 miles to Abya, on the railway, and there found a damp which Div had left deliberately for such as us. There were no boots or shoes to fit me, but I found three pairs of socks, and we found some food. We were just preparing to cook it when a party of Burma Frontier Force under Capt Edwards turned up: so we joined forces with them, and the following day continued our march. When we had done 13 miles, to Waw, we saw a real sight for tired eyes - the leading tanks of the 7th Armoured Brigade. With them was a battalion of Cameronians who were later to become great friends of mine in 111 Bde of the Chindits. They did us proud, and after hot tea and sausages, we were lorried to Pegu. The worst part of all of that was turning up minus arms and equipment, even though it wasn't my fault.

Tail piece to Sittang

I have seen it in print that "the Sittang crossing made Dunkirk look like a picnic." After a lie as terrifying and stupendous as this, mere words cease to have any meaning. It stands in my memory as the supreme and sublime example of the ultimate in hysterical exaggeration. It was written by a woman.

Pegu to Rangoon

My time with 4th Burma Rifles was nearly at an end. We soon marched back to a village some 20 miles along the link road, and from there the Battalion was ordered up to Mandalay for L of C duties. I had already applied for transfer to Commandos, and just as the battalion was about to move off a demand came in for two Burmese interpreters to go to a new Brigade just about to land. That I thought offered better prospects than going north: so Hugo Hinds and I each took a fond farewell of the battalion; and on March 3rd met 63 Bde as they landed in Rangoon.

63 Independent Infantry Brigade

63 Bde landed on March 3rd, under the command of Brig. Wickham. They consisted of 1/11th Sikhs, 1/10th Gurkhas and 2/13th Frontier Force Rifles. They were a fine lot, and we were mightily glad to see them. We were glad to see the large amount of up-to-date equipment and lorries which they brought, though they were to lose 9/10ths of it within a week. Like all other battalions at this time, they had a large number of recruits, but none the less they had a fine record. I was interpreter to Bde HQ, Hugo Hinds and the other two Burma Rifle officers being with the three battalions.

We went straight up to Hlawga and encamped with our mountain of stores beside the lake. I paid one last visit to Rangoon, on about March 5th, to try and do some shopping, and that was my last glimpse of Rangoon until May 4th 1945. During this time the Japanese were attacking in the Pegu area, and it was already known Rangoon was going to have to be abandoned. Nobody, however, had any realisation of just how fast the Japanese were going to move, and it was this fact which was largely responsible for our Brigade suffering a most serious setback. With a view to getting things on the move, the Brigadier with the Brigade Major, three COs and their Adjutants, went, on March 5th, up the Pegu road to reconnoitre an area possible for training. They went in two armoured cars, the particular type we had having open tops. It is difficult to see they could have taken more reasonable precautions, but as it turned out, they'd have been far better in staff cars. A Jap sniper up a tree with an LMG put a burst into each armoured car, which then, of course, became deathtraps, as the bullets, which would have gone straight through the floor of a staff car, went flying round inside. The Brigadier was wounded (lost one eye) and was out for the campaign, the BM was slightly wounded and was out for two months, two COs were killed and one badly wounded and one Adjutant wounded. So before going into battle - which we were to do two days later, the entire command altered. Not a very good start. And so we come to the memorable battle of Taukkyan, a battle almost without precedent, I should think, and the last stage in my education in the fog of war. I don't think I've learnt much about the fog of war since then, but Taukkyan was a fitting headstone to a building whose foundations were firmly laid at Kawkareik, and whose stately and graceful pillars were raised up at Kyaitko and Sittang.

To understand the battle of Taukkyan it is necessary to understand something about the general situation. There had been a very bloody battle at Pegu, one of the bitterest of the war, and our troops were withdrawing down the road from Pegu to the Prome road junction. Meanwhile, it had been decided to abandon Rangoon, and all that was

left in Rangoon was coming up the Prome Road - and the whole bash
met at the T road. I have made a sketch map. This is not to scale, and
only the salient features have been shown. The distance from Rangoon
to the T is about 22 miles, from Pegu to the T is about 45, from the T to
the roadblock is about six, and from Hlawga to the T is also about six.
From the T up to the block there is jungle on both sides of the road.

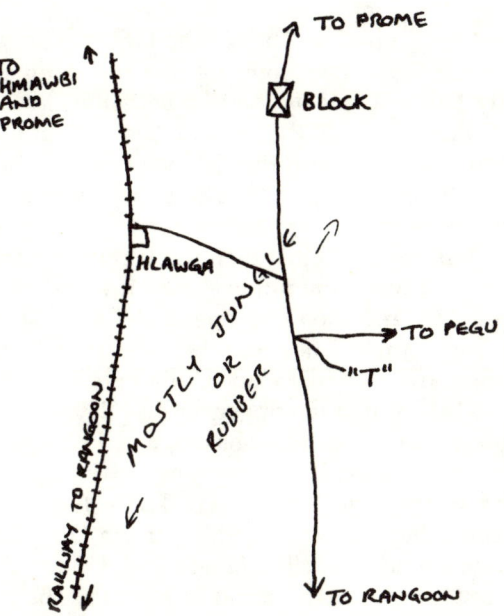

Now I may get a day out over my dates, but the sequence of events
will be right. I left Hlawga - which was left in the charge of a base
party - on 6th March, and had been put in charge of the Bde HQ
defence platoon. We got to the T at about 6 pm, to find the most
almighty traffic jam you'd ever want to see. However, the CO of the
Duke of Wellington's (name forgotten, but a very fine man who was
subsequently killed) had taken charge and was straightening things out
fast. We were told to spend the night in the village, which we did.

The day after - 7th - we were to move off north, but not at crack of
dawn. The defence platoon was told to stay behind, me with it, while
the three battalions went off ahead. It was on that day I witnessed one
of the most awe-inspiring sights of the war. At 8 am what I looked like
a colossal black thunder cloud came up. By noon it was overhead, and
by dusk was on the far horizon. As one looked at Rangoon, therefore,
at dusk, the whole of the sky to one's left was coal black, and the half
to one's right clear blue, and it looked as if a knife had cut the sky in

half. It was, of course, Syriam but it was pretty remarkable that even at a range of 25 miles the smoke should have blotted out half the sky. A truly frightening sight.

At about 3 o'clock we were told that the troops moving north had met a roadblock and were trying to break it. There was nobody to give me any orders at this time: so I thought we might as well move up and join in the fun. What had actually happened was that our Brigade, plus the Gloucesters, who were not in our Brigade, had attacked the roadblock and failed to break it. The two battalions who were attacking on the flanks, incidentally, had both got lost in the jungle. There had been some pretty heavy losses by the two battalions in the centre - the Gloucesters and the 2/13th FFR - and blokes, not unnaturally, were somewhat shaken. I arrived with the defence platoon about dusk, and went up to see who I could report to. The first person I met was Hugo Hinds, badly wounded in the leg. I went forward to try and get some transport to take him back and just then the Japanese started firing. We had to take cover, and when the fun was over it was dark. I went to see who I could report to, and then had one of the nastiest experiences of the war. Seeing my Burma Rifles hat, they assumed I was a Burman, and the next thing I knew I had a loaded rifle in the middle of my chest and the Sikh who held it had his finger on the trigger. I told them who I was, but morale by then was a bit shaken, and I was put under arrest and had my rifle taken away. It was in many ways the most unpleasant experience I had in the war. They didn't know I still had two hand grenades: so I could have done something if the Japs had attacked. It was not a night for sound sleep. The Japanese did not make any serious effort to attack, but sent in small patrols to jitter us. The procedure was as follows: The Japs threw in a couple of fire crackers: the troops fired 500 rounds into the jungle at nothing. The Japs waited half an hour and threw in two more: the troops fired 500 more rounds at nothing - and so on.

March 8th at 6 am did not present a pleasing prospect. The Japs had a block north of us, Rangoon was gone behind us, and we seemed to be caught if we couldn't break out. An attack was prepared for 2 am and we were told, incredible though it may sound, that if the attack failed we should all probably be captured! Nice thought.

At about 12.30, a liaison officer came up from the rear, looking for the forward troops, went too far in his jeep and before he knew where he was found himself up against what looked uncommonly like a roadblock. Needless to say, he turned round pretty quickly, and was astonished not to be fired at. So he went back and told the management he didn't think the block was held. Needless to say, he was told not to be such a B.F. and it was pointed out what a splendid position the Japs had to catch us. However, he persisted, and so the management sent up a couple of tanks to investigate. These confirmed that the block was no longer held. This, needless to say, caused general astonishment in the ranks of the management - and others, but not so much as when another officer came in to report that about a Japanese division was marching in threes, in broad daylight, down the middle of the railway line, some two miles away. It was immediately assumed, of course, that this bloke had received severe cranial injuries, but he too persisted, so once more the management sent out emissaries to verify this astounding state of affairs, and there they saw the Japanese 55th Div, headed by it's Lt.-Gen OC making good time in threes down the railway line. So, while the Japs were making good time down the line, all of us, Jeeps, tanks, mules, marching troops, staff cars, 3-tonners, 25-pdrs. etc. all mashed together, went milling up the road.

And that is the true story of the battle of Taukkyan roadblock. The *Illustrated London News* had a slightly varied story whereby we "smashed our way through with tank support and escaped to the north" - and beautifully illustrated it was too - the only snag was that it never happened.

It may be of interest here to explain what did in fact happen, as this is now known. The Japanese attack on Burma, up, at any rate, to the fall of Rangoon, was on a timed programme, and the GOC 55th Div, largely owing to the bloody battle of Pegu, was a day late. He was informed that if he did not get to Rangoon on the day he was supposed to, he would have failed in his duty to the Emperor, and would, presumably have had to commit Mati Hari. He obviously didn't fancy busting across the triangle for fear of a further clash with our forces; so he put down a block north of Taukkyan, not to catch us, but merely to prevent us hitting him on the flank as we went north. He then marched round behind his own roadblock, and when his whole division was clear, pulled in the road block and went full bat for Rangoon, thus making up the day lost.

We reached Hmawbi in the dark, our objective for the night being the village of Wantchaung some six miles north of Hmawbi. The road from Hmawbi, like in most places in lower Burma, is banked up with rain trees over it, and the management decided it would be too dangerous for us to march along it for fear of being outlined to any enemy patrols. The tanks, guns etc. had to go along the road, but we were to go through the six miles of paddy which separated us from our objective. We started off by selecting about the only paddy field in Burma - the Government Farm - which had a fence round it, and there was a delay while that was knocked down. We then executed a manoeuvre I don't ever expect to see again - we drew up a division in MASS - i.e., a brigade in threes. Then off we moved. The obvious thing to do, of course, was to keep 200 yards from the road, which was gloriously outlined, and you couldn't go wrong. Not a bit of it! Compasses are given to you in the army for marching with at night, so that's what we were to do. I told the bloke concerned what would happen, and it wasn't long before it did - viz the road bent slightly, and the leading units of the right hand brigade found themselves being caught up in bamboo, or spiked on cactus or in danger of taking a header down the well of the garden into which we had strayed. So the division had to about turn, 200 yards back, 200 yards to the right, right turn and begin again. We were going fearfully slowly and getting very tired. At about ten to four we sat down for our halt, and the bloke leading the div went to sleep - and so did all the rest of us! We woke at 5.30, a division in paddy fields, dawn breaking and the Japs with air superiority. We DID move then, and reached our village as fast as we could, but not before a Lysander had come over. Of course, it got shot up, but luckily was not hit.

That morning they sent lorries for us, and that evening we were at Tharrawaddy, with 75 miles between us and the Japanese.

My education was complete.

Tharrawaddy to Kalewa

After the much shorter legs which I had been dealing with hitherto, this will strike the reader as a somewhat extended one: but really, once Rangoon was lost, there was a monotonous, and, it seemed, almost inexorable sameness about the rest of the campaign. We now know from study of the Japanese High Command's grand strategic plan, that they (1) expected Singapore to hold out for a year; (2) only wanted to capture Rangoon, not Burma, with a view to preventing supplies going through to China, as it would have been, the besieged fortress of Singapore; (3) were going to give back Burma at the peace conference, as stage one in the 100 years' war only contemplated permanent retention of countries as far west as Malaya inclusive. That explains why the Japanese were so strict about the prevention of looting, arson etc. in Malaya, while permitting looting both by Japanese soldiers and locals in Burma.

What the Japanese expected us to do I don't know - surrender, presumably, or apply for life (?) membership of the Mata-hari club. Anyway, it is clear from the few days respite we had after Taukkyan that they were not immediately prepared to pursue us to the north. When they did, they followed their usual tactics of outflanking, threatening encirclement by road block, and we, being roadbound, had either to withdraw before being encircled, or else had to hack a way through the roadblocks with loss of life and equipment. The one or two attempts to take the initiative on a big scale were vitiated by jealousies and suspicions between us and the Chinese, with the Americans between the two of us, and there is no object in re-hashing the sorry tale here.

Soon after Tharrawaddy, at Chepo, I was made staff captain of 63 Brigade, as the Brigadier said he couldn't stand the other any longer. Normally a staff captain's job is largely a coggage one, forms, forms and more forms, but I saw the job under the best conditions. It was no use sending in indents for stores, clothing etc. which didn't exist, nor a whole mass of daily returns on which no action could be taken in any event: so I was able to concentrate on essentials and quite soon my job boiled down to a few really essential returns: water, food, transport and ammunition. That gave me quite a bit of time for nosing around - I had a jeep - and I was able to keep in touch with Div personally and find out when an extra issue of, say, clothing, was likely to be available. On one occasion I went on a trek through the village in front of our position by day to tell the villagers about reporting Japs (I was the only Burmese speaker in the Bde) and on my return found that one of the forward companies had not been warned and that I had spent ten minutes in the sights of a Bren gun.

I don't propose to recount all the places we stopped at - and doubt if I could remember them all, but Chepo and Putsu were two of our longest, but it was not long before we were back in Prome. This, as stated, was necessitated by the constant threats of Japanese encirclement, and the most sickening and heartbreaking part of the whole show was to be constantly withdrawing WITHOUT FIGHTING.

Prome we really did think was going to be a bastion, and we were looking forward to a good battle there. We stayed there for about a week, and were there for Easter. The flies were past belief when we first arrived, but the Japs bombed and burnt the bazaar and thereafter the flies became vastly less. The Japanese, of course, were not idle, and to show the arrogance of some of them, one afternoon we looked out across the river and - in broad daylight - saw some Japs wheeling a 70mm gun over the sandbank with a view to having a few pots at us, presumably. As our HQ, the DC's bungalow was on the telephone to the 25-pdrs., which were about half a mile away, we had the gratifying sight of seeing the second salvo get about three direct hits and the whole gun crew disintegrate. Prome was one of the few places where the Japs attacked early in the night as opposed to doing an approach march by night and attacking shortly before dawn. In a sense it was hardly a night attack, as the moon (a full one) was so brilliant that it was almost a day attack. We were hoping for a good bloody battle, and I believe we could have given them heavy losses, but news came that another column had crossed from west to east to the north os us: so our rear was threatened and out we got - in the night.

We next took up positions south of Allanmyo, and soon after that moved back to Taungdwingyi.

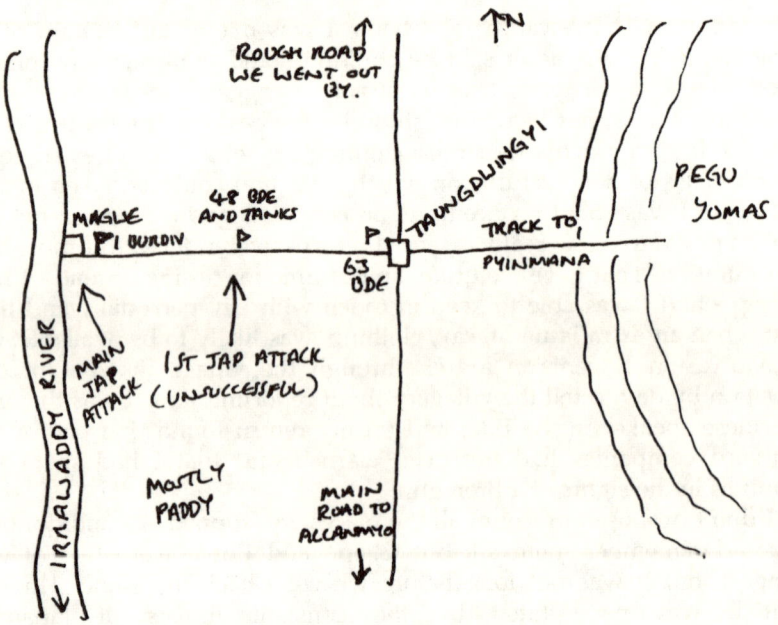

Taungdwingyi, in my opinion, was a real finish of the campaign. Rangoon probably decided the issue, admittedly, but Taungdwingyi put the matter beyond all shadow of doubt. To illustrate this I have made another sketch map, which once more is not to scale and only the salient points are shown. At this time the Chinese were level with us at Pyinmana. After we had settled down at Taungdwingyi, we had a visit from no less a person than Slim, who was then GOC BURCORPS, and who addressed officers. The following was the burden of his remarks:

> You've probably been wondering why we have had these everlasting withdrawals, and I sympathise with you. I've loathed them too. The reason, however, is that I must have good open country where the tanks can operate with good effect against the Japs, and this is it. And this is my plan: You, 63 Bde, are to hold Taungdwingyi, 1 BURDIV is in Magwe, 48 Bde and the Tanks are in the middle. Now, wherever the Japs attack, the other two will close in, and we'll really knock him this time.

I don't remember feeling more elated in the whole campaign than I did that day. Thank God, we all thought, now we know what is expected of us. We had plenty of food, plenty of sleep and rest, and were there for about ten days. Apart from one Jap raid we were beautifully peaceful. In that raid, incidentally, I saw the only aircraft I've ever seen brought down, hit by a Bofors, and it burst into flames; a good sight.

Then the Japs attacked. They went for 48 Bde first, got no change out of them, and sheered off to go for 1 BURDIV. Here we go boys - and we were just waiting for orders to attack. Orders came - to withdraw without firing to a new line. That was the end. Before that the management had always been able to make out there was some special reason why we had to pull out, but not this time. We knew the plan, we had the troops, ammunition etc. and the necessary conditions for Slim's plan to operate obtained, yet we were pulling out: and it was after Taungdwingyi that nobody really had any serious doubts that we were on our way to India.

Why didn't we attack? We were all sure it would have worked at the time and I still believe it would have had a good chance. It wasn't Slim's fault, actually, it was all owing to the wrangles with the Chinese, and Slim was overruled from higher up. The Chinese were so browned off that they had made it a test of faith that we should not leave Taungdwingyi until they had taken it over. They never did turn up to take it over, and as a result Alexander would not let us leave our positions to attack the Japs for fear of even worse rows with the Chinese. That was the story we heard at the time, and from talks I have had since with senior officers, I still believe it to be substantially true. But it was the last blow.

There was some pretty bad going from Taungdwingyi to the lateral road from Meiktila to Kyaukpadaung, but the Sappers, who did wonderful work throughout the campaign, had got some sort of a road through, and it was good enough for MT. From Taungdwingyi to Kalewa was the most exhausting part of the campaign. It was getting very hot, and withdrawals were more or less continuous. My standard day was something as follows:

Being Staff Captain I was responsible for the transport, and also for getting back ahead of the marching troops to have food and camp (?) ready. So I'd move off after dark in my jeep, no lights, and the convoy following as close as possible. The normal jump was about 20 miles and one way or another this seldom took less than six or seven hours. Max speed in any case was only about eight mph, and once an hour one had to go back and check the convoy. There were always three or four breakdowns of one sort or another during the night. By the time we had selected the site, got the vehicles under cover and seen about food the marching troops were in, and had to be shown to their areas. Some sort of a meal, and then an attempt to get some sleep. By 2 pm there were usually orders out for a further withdrawal, and so the process was repeated. During the last 30 days I had four full nights sleep. The rest I reckon I averaged three-and-a-half hours asleep in the 24.

We spent two days on the Meiktila-Kyaukpadaung road at a big chaung some 20 miles from Meiktila, and from there were going to go up to Myingyan. They scratched this fixture, however, and we were to go up to Myitnge, which also involved going through Meiktila. One of the places where we stopped for a day was some five miles north of Meiktila, and I spent a somewhat different day - we were machine-gunned from the air - from the previous time I'd been there, which was the first day of my honeymoon when my wife and I had stopped for a picnic lunch. We got two more nights at Myitnge, and then off again - over the Ava bridge, and thence to Monywa. This was the last brush we had with the Japanese, who had taken Monywa and we failed to dislodge them. So we destroyed all our heavy transport - we hadn't much by then, and marched round Monywa in the night. A day at Alon, and then north once more. The road proper stopped at Kaduma, and from there on we went by roads and tracks made by the Sappers. I ran into Rodney Drake at Shwegyin and we had a meal together, and then I was sent across to Kalewa. If my memory is correct, I crossed the Chindwin on 10th May, and went flat-down with malaria. I filtered back to Tamu, Palel, Imphal - which was in a fearful mess having been bombed that morning - to Dimapur. At that time there were no hospitals worth the name, no drugs and thousands of people pouring through every day. Finally I decided to go back to Imphal where at any rate I knew I'd get food, and a couple of days later I was back there. The Burma Campaign was over.

There were many reasons why we lost the Burma Campaign, and there's no object in retailing the whole lot, but in my opinion far and away the most important point was that the Japs were trained for jungle war and we were not, and nothing - air support friendly inhabitants, or anything else, would have made any difference as long as that fact remained. If men are wrongly trained, bravery will only be a palliative, not a cure. Considering all things the morale of the troops remained amazingly high right through, as is shown by Kyaukse when 48 Bde attacked and killed 400 Japs counted for the loss of four dead themselves. But things being as they were it is hard to see how the final result could have been very difficult.

One rather amusing thing happened in the hills during the retreat. In the later stages, several parties were coming through the Naga Hills from Homalin and such places. On the west of the river, in addition to the Nagas, parties of the Assam Rifles were doing what they could to help in the refugees. As anyone who knows the East is aware, there are rest houses in such places as the Naga Hills, primarily for government servants on tour, but also for civilians if any, and of course these rest houses were used by the refugees who passed through. All rest houses have a book, so that those who stay in them can record the fact to enable the inspecting officer when he comes to check the cash taken by the rest house keeper etc. Needless to say, on the occasion of the retreat certain of the guests tried to get some amusement (it can't have been too easy in those wretched conditions) by making entries which were not strictly accurate, and two men had signed themselves as under

NAME	NATIONALITY	BUSINESS
Adolf Hitler	German	Espionage
Hidekei Tojo	Japanese	Ditto

The next visitor to the rest house was the Subedar Major of the Assam Rifles plus a party, and in the course of his duties he inspected the book. He could hardly believe his eyes! HITLER *AND* TOJO! It couldn't be! Look again - it WAS. The greatest event that had ever happened in the Naga Hills, and he was the man who had discovered it! This was practically a signed armistice by Germany and Japan. Get these men and the greatest war in the world's history was over. It was too late to move that night, but he had the priceless document sewn up in groundsheets, and the morning after he and his two fastest riflemen, stripped of all bar absolute essentials - with the Armistice of course - set out for Imphal. They did 30 miles a day over mountain tracks for three days on end, and arrived at 4 Corps HQ absolutely exhausted. Would any of you have had the heart to tell him? I wouldn't have had.

No account of the retreat from Burma could be complete without mention being made of the Assam tea planters association. They organised cooly labour, made roads, established refugee camps, built bashas and worked day and night to help the unfortunate refugees and also the army. Not only the men but also their wives threw themselves into the breach, and there must be several thousands alive today who'd have gone under but for the voluntary and unstinted help of these men and women. They received entirely inadequate official recognition.

2
Kohima Interlude

We were not to stay very long at Imphal. While there, Wavell came and gave us all a talk, which was illuminating and encouraging. I had met him once before when he came down and shook hands with all officers at Thaton. It was wisely (?) decided he must have air cover in case Imphal was raided: he had it - ONE HURRICANE. However, either the Jap fifth column didn't get the news through or the Japs weren't interested, for we were not troubled. Our next move, in June, was to Kohima, and I went on with a small advanced party, reaching there on 3rd June. I liked Kohima from the first moment I clapped eyes on it, as the first sight I saw was a Naga with a full basket of plums on his back. One of our most crying needs had been fruit for the last few weeks, and I could hardly believe my eyes: still less for the price of Rs. 2/8 for the whole basket! I didn't bargain boys: I gave him 10 Rupees for good measure and ate 34 that afternoon.

Apart from war leave up to Lansdowne, Kohima was to be my home for the rest of 1942, and a more delightful place you could never wish to see. It stands on the road from Dimapur to Imphal at mile 46 from Dimapur, and is 4600 feet up. The scenery is as fine as one could want, with the jungle covered hills rising up to 9890 feet - Mount Japvo - and in the cold weather the snows of the Himalayas, 180 miles to the north, stand out clear as crystal. But to me, one of the chief beauties of Kohima is the terraces, and to see, at paddy harvest, those golden-covered terraces rising tier after tier, up the sides of the hills, the tops being covered in jungle, is a sight I shall never forget. The Nagas, I can say without hesitation, have, in my opinion, the highest moral standards of any people I have met in the East. I do not only refer to sexual morality, but to the much wider moral outlook, honesty, truthfulness, doing what they say they will and the like. And not only that, they are always cheerful and smiling, and their lurid, if scanty! clothing makes them appear even more so. I can strongly advise anyone who wants a trip which, in peace time at any rate, was off the beaten track, to go there. The average Bengali lawyer, say, who has probably the lowest moral standard of any living human being, regards the Nagas as a sort of semi-animal. But in the sight of God the Naga is as much above the Bengali lawyer as his glorious hills are higher than the evil smelling streets of that sink of iniquity Calcutta. The Nagas are kindly, simple, unspoiled people, and it was a joy to be with them.

In peacetime Kohima's only white inhabitants were the officers of the Assam Rifles, the District Commissioner and the American Missionary and his family. No account of our stay in Kohima would be complete without a word about these latter two.

Charles Pawsey, Indian Civil Service, the DC at Kohima stands in my memory as the best example I have seen of all that is good in the ICS. He was DC of all the Naga Hills and I'll wager there were few villages in the hills he didn't know. He had the advantage of being responsible only to the Governor of Assam, and not to the Government of Assam, and so was not inundated by the waves of useless forms, returns, reports etc. which have broken the heart of many a good man in other branches of the Indian and Burma Civil Services. But that by itself would not have been enough to account for his tremendous influence for good in the hills.

To find the reason for that, one had to know Charles Pawsey himself. A man of uncompromising uprightness, his one great love was the Nagas, and he didn't just know them in his office in Kohima: he knew them in their villages - for no amount of paperwork prevented him from touring in the hills, (although he was not able to go on doing this during the war, when an army was using the road) meeting his Nagas, helping them with their problems and generally being their father. And as such they regarded him - for they knew that from him they would always get justice, sympathy and help, no matter how much personal trouble it was to him. And the proof came when the Japanese broke into the Naga Hills and all but took Kohima. Not one Naga turned fifth columnist. Under Charles Pawsey's direction, and often at great risk to themselves, the Nagas, who were completely loyal, ran messages through the Jap lines, delivered, under orders, false information to the Japanese, kept us informed of what the enemy was doing and generally assisted in every way. Charles Pawsey himself, meanwhile, was at his post, and had the sorrowful experience of seeing his house - in which he had been so charming a host to so many of us - captured by the Japanese, and then blown to dust and splinters by two squadrons of dive-bombers and an hour's shelling by medium artillery. He received the CIE for his services - less than he deserved - which he could add to the MC and bar which he won in the First World War. To those who criticise our colonial administration I would say "Go and see Charles Pawsey."

The other man who deserves mention was the American Baptist Missionary, Mr Supplee, who with his wife and two youngest children, Joan aged 16 and Bob aged about 13, lived in Kohima and also had a Mission church and school. He had been 20-odd years in the Naga hills, and had certainly found his calling. He used to tour everywhere on a specially constructed motor bicycle, which would take himself and two others, and he managed to get to some truly remarkable places on it. He also was a very great help to the army, and had great influence amongst the Nagas, by whom he was much respected. As Brigade IO it was my duty to find out as much about the Nagas as I could, and he was not only a great help, but also a very good friend to me. His entire Mission buildings were reduced to ruins in the fighting, but his influence for good amongst the Nagas will be none the less for that. He and his family, however, had gone on leave to America some time before the battle of Kohima began.[1]

Typical of the sort of way the Government of India treated the Naga Hills was the following. Many thousands of refugees, when coming out of Burma, came through the Naga hills. The Nagas helped them as much as possible, and in many villages gave the refugees so much food that by the rains of 1942 their own stocks of rice were dangerously low. As the new crop was not due in until December, more rice had to be sent to them, and this could only be obtained from India. The Indian Government sent rice up to Kohima, but made it quite clear the Nagas had to pay for it! (I suppose just to show them that if they insist on helping British and Indian refugees to safety they must expect to incur severe penalties.) Not being a man for disobeying official orders Charles Pawsey charged them for their rice - price one anna per bag, including carriage, which was charged to the Government of India!

It is hard to exaggerate the confusion there was on the Eastern front in June 1942. We had just been knocked sideways in the Burma campaign, and nobody was sure the Japanese were not coming on after us straightaway. Had they done so, I don't know what would have happened, as the morale of the troops, though not nearly as low as some made out, was not high, and the weapon and ammunition position was far from good. The Burma Campaign had shown that none of our troops were properly trained for jungle warfare, and that, of course, was also true of such reserves as there were behind us in India. But the most serious part was the supply. The road from Dimapur (the railhead) to Imphal was 133 miles long, and of that all but nine miles at the Dimapur end and 14 miles at the Imphal end was over hill section. The road had been built for single track traffic, and

---

1   Mr Supplee had educated his four children - I only met the two younger ones - in the Mission school at Kohima, as a result of which all four spoke absolutely perfect Angami Naga as well as English. I asked him if being educated with Nagas had not tended to retard his own children's education? He told me that so far from that, he considered that given equal chances an average Naga child was as intelligent as, if not more intelligent than, an average American child of the same age.

was normally used by about six vehicles only. It now found itself the only supply route for a small army. It was subject to landslides throughout its length, and in one place, as will shortly be seen, regularly bogged every year. Our transport was not enough, and the unfortunate Indian drivers had been trained on 15 cwts in the plains. They found themselves driving 3-tonners in rain and mist, largely in the dark, on a one-way road which would have been a passing out test for a British grade A driver. As the final blow, they were - inevitably - so overworked that many crashed their lorries by simply falling asleep at the wheel. In the circumstances these drivers - almost all Indian - did a magnificent job of work, and were a most important factor in the success of the whole show. Nevertheless, between May and the end of December 1942, 800 3-ton lorries went over the khud between Dimapur and Imphal.

If possible, things were worst behind. Dimapur, I feel sure would have been the spot chosen as our base by Tojo or Hitler. It was, when we arrived, under the undisputed and absolute rule of King Anopheles the First. In low, swampy jungle-covered country, it was supposed to be the worst spot in all India for malaria, and I can well believe it. The figures of malaria casualties were almost beyond belief. I don't know who claimed the palm, but it lay between the Nepalese unit and a company of the RIASC. The former base their claim on the grounds that during the rains of 1942 their unit had 750% malaria, i.e., every man averaged seven-and-a-half goes of malaria that rains, and that they reached the stage where they could only march two miles: over that distance the sweat and exhaustion brought malaria on once more. The company of the RIASC claim that at one time every single man, officer and follower were in hospital with malaria and a local unit had to send in guards for their stores until they had enough men to guard them themselves. I leave the reader to hand the palm. The army malariologists were sent for and were asked what they could do about it. They replied they could fix it if they were given absolute carte blanche, and were allowed to proceed with no interference on tactical or camouflage grounds. This was given and in the cold weather of 1942-1943 they went to work. Malaria figures in 1943 were 15% - a remarkable performance. In this connection, I think it is not fairly realised how much our ultimate success was owing to the work of the medical and allied services. We had the very best of everything - once we had got going - and the ability of the medicals to help such a large proportion of our men in the field in such unhealthy regions was one of the prime match-winning factors of the war, and I should like to pay my humble but sincere tribute to those services who did so much for us.

The railway from Dimapur to Gauhati was, of course, totally

inadequate for supplying us properly, only ever having been designed as a subsidiary line: and in addition to us it had the troops further north to cope with. then there was the bottleneck of the Brahmaputra river between Gauhati and Pandu. On top of that were the damned swine in congress who by train-wrecking and general sabotage did their level best to betray India to the Japanese for their own personal ends, and had we not had, in Lord Linlithgow, a viceroy who had guts enough to put the leaders inside, the whole of India would have gone up in smoke behind us. To cap everything, in June there was an abnormal rise on one of the feeder streams of the Brahmaputra, and the mighty, roaring flood, picked up a steel railway bridge and deposited it some 50 yards downstream.

It will be appreciated, therefore, that all we could do was to keep the forward troops supplied, in order to resist any further Japanese advance, but at the same time to hope one wouldn't take place. The commanders on the spot found themselves having to have a fair number of troops for normal guard duties, and knowing that if they tried any elaborate training during the rains with troops already in need of rest and leave, they would merely be inviting still more casualties.

We didn't always make things as easy as they could be. Charles Pawsey told me one story as follows: In June 1942 a particular army unit was in an area where firewood was plentiful, and had to be supplied with firewood as part of its normal "Q" requirements. They were being supplied by a superior formation whose powers of local purchase did not extend to their area, though in addition to firewood there were plenty of Nagas to cut it. The firewood was, therefore, bought locally in the superior formation's area where, incidentally, it was scarce, but where - blessed dispensation - they were authorised to buy the firewood. It was then lorried 20 miles up the road, the lorries returning empty! This when we were frantic for transport. Pawsey had to take this to the Corps Commander before he got it put right.

As stated, before this lengthy but necessary digression, we arrived in Kohima early in June and were billeted as best we could. The 1/11th Sikhs were some six miles out to the east, under tents, the 1/10th GR at mile 42 (i.e. four miles down the road) in tents, the Gloucesters were in the Assam Rifles lines, in Kohima itself (the 2/13th FFR had left us in June, the Gloucesters replacing them), and Bde HQ was in the gaol. It was a good solid if somewhat unimaginative structure, but it suited our purposes excellently. Being Staff Captain, I was able to choose my own abode and without hesitation chose the condemned cell, spending longer in it that the type of person for whom it was originally built - and probably in considerably greater comfort.

I should have added one important point. Early in June the Brigadier of 63 Bde, A.E.Barlow MC, gave up his appointment. He had taken over after Taukyan, and had commanded our brigade throughout the campaign. He was a thoroughly sound, if not brilliant officer, and we all had confidence in him. He was a very good friend to me, and I was very sorry when I heard he had been killed in a motor smash in Chowringee in the early part of this year - 1946. His place was taken by W.D.A.Lentaigne, CIE, DSO, of whom I shall have much more to say. In my opinion he was, and still is a brilliant officer, and is one of the best friends I have made out of this war. I myself gave up the post of Staff Captain in June and took over the appointment of Brigade Intelligence Officer.

There wasn't really much work to do of great importance. There was some enciphering and deciphering, keeping up a battle map, and the various other routine jobs which fall to the lot of a Bde IO, but that was about all. At the end of July I went on my 31 days war leave.

During this time one of the sights in our part of the world was to go and see the famous Mile 42, which was four miles below us on the Dimapur side. In June this place became impassable, as about 100 yards of road became bog, and the whole hillside started slipping down into the valley. It wasn't a landslide in the sense that a whole lot of rock came crashing down. That happened in plenty of places, but could be cleared. This was a question of a whole section of a hill becoming liquid mud and just slipping - slowly. We asked the civil what they normally did about it and they said "wait for the end of the rains. This happens every year, but this year is a month earlier than usual. As we have only six vehicles normally it doesn't worry us." A nice state of affairs. They tried everything. They put boards across and had thousands of coolys ferrying cargo. Then they devised a system whereby with steel mesh they could - by working like maniacs for 18 hours - get it to stand up for six hours, and it was a curious sight on, say, Sunday, to see Saturday's road 15 feet below you, Friday's 15 feet below that, and so on. They finally got at the root of the trouble, two small streams which flowed under the hill starting from the top. They diverted those, and after shifting tens of thousands of tons of rock and earth, made a permanently stable piece of road. Work was, of course, going on everywhere else to widen the road, and before the end of the war it was a magnificent, two-way, all weather road, probably the finest of its kind in India. Tens of thousands of Nagas were, of course, necessary for this, and in this Charles Pawsey was absolutely invaluable.

I had a very pleasant leave at Lansdowne, seeing my daughter for the first time, the only snag being that both my wife and I, when we went down to Delhi, got malaria. That made me a week late in returning, and my orders were to report to Gaya, some 200 miles west of Calcutta.

Gaya rest camp was one of the biggest shocks of the war, and was symptomatic, though I hope not typical of the utter chaos all along our L of C at this time. The camp - just tents in a field - was some six miles outside the town. On arrival, I reported to a bloke who seemed to be in charge of the camp, and asked when I would be able to leave, and received a reply somewhat as follows: "Ask me another. I arrived here six weeks ago, and after making strong, but unavailing efforts to get out, three weeks ago they arbitrarily took me onto the camp staff, and here I am. I may be here for life." I debated whether to make a quick bolt for it, but was finally restrained on being assured that I would be allowed to go three days later. That camp was a scandal. The CO lived in Gaya and never came anywhere near the place: his adjutant came down once a day with orders. For the rest it was left to run itself. Small wonder, therefore, that when the camp was finally cleared up they found 2000 Indian other ranks in it who were not even on the books. It was too easy. They reported, were told by a harassed officer to go and get some khana, and all they had to do then was to do nothing: the camp never caught up with them, and they were perfectly covered: they had reported as ordered. I heard the CO took felt on that one - he richly deserved it.

Later on the rest camps and transit camps were one of the very best features of the whole L of C. Even at the start Dimapur was good, chiefly because it was run by a Lt.-Col. Blackburn, who was not only a man of drive and sense, but also sympathy, who realised blokes out of the line wanted a bit of comfort. Too old for command in the front line, men of this type did a job of work far more valuable than many would recognise. I've certainly been grateful to Blackburn and others like him on many occasions.

I left Gaya (and hope I never see it again) in charge of a train with 750 men of 39 separate units on board, some having only one or two men. My 'adjutant' was an old Burma Campaign friend, Captain B.H.Darley of 1/3rd GR and we had two other officers. The trip took three days and we only lost two men between Gaya and Dimapur. That time we went up the river for 24 hours from Dhubri. I asked what rations the ship had on board and was told none. What I wasn't told was that there was no fresh water either. So the Brahmaputra had to deputise.

Things were much more promising when I got back to Kohima in mid-September. the Japanese had not attacked, supplies were much better, the rains were tailing off, and there was a general feeling that the worst was over. We moved out into the jungle, and after the whole Bde had been 'blanketed,' i.e. given the full malaria course to clear us up we started training. In addition to training ourselves we had the Commando platoons (two at a time) of the nine battalions in the all-British 70th Division to train. I found myself giving a large number of lectures, both to these men and to my own Bde Intelligence Section, acted as umpire on jungle schemes, and generally got about quite a bit. In the glorious weather and country it was grand fun, and we felt at last we were going to get somewhere. With Hugh Pettigrew, who, like myself, can't see a hill without wanting to go up it, I climbed Mount Japvo one Sunday and got one of the best views I've ever had anywhere.

There had been several changes in the Bde, the 1/11th Sikhs had gone, their place being taken by the 1/3rd GR, and there had been several changes on the Bde staff. We were, however, a very happy lot and got on very well together. We also got on very well with the Commando Battalion of the Black Watch when they gave their halloween party around a camp fire, and it was on the morning after that I took my great oath to have my next drink in Mandalay or Rangoon, and except for one rum, I was uncompromisingly teetotal for 15 months, though I admit I'd thought - and hoped - we were going back to Burma a bit sooner than that!

We left Kohima on New Year's Day 1943, to march to Imphal, and we hoped Mandalay, having spent what was for me, in many ways, the pleasantest months of the war.

Imphal

We took four days - or rather nights - to march to Imphal, and when we got there were billeted in Imphal itself for a bit. I had just previously been told to report to Eastern Army as an IO, but the Bde, with the help of Corps, had blown this down, thereby doing me out of the first Chindit show, I now know, though I didn't at the time. We fiddled about at Imphal for about three weeks, and then went down to a new camp at MS 44 on the Tiddim Road, where we did further training. I now know that when we went down to Imphal it *was* the intention to make a limited advance as far as the Chindwin that cold weather: in fact the orders were actually typed out. But at the last moment everything bar the Chindits was cancelled: so that was that.

In February Lentaigne left us to form a new brigade on Chindit lines, and I applied to go with him as, together with a good many others, I despaired of ever seeing action on the 4 Corps front. This Major-Gen. Cowan DSO, GOC 17 Div, refused to countenance. The new brigadier was a superb man too, Brig. A.E. Cumming, VC, OBE, MC, having won his VC in Malaya, and we got on extremely well together. However, training did not last for long there, as the whole Bde was ordered back for a rains rest at Shillong. We got settled in there and were just beginning some training when the Japanese attacked in the Chin Hills, and the whole Bde, less the Gloucesters, who were leaving us, were ordered back to the Chin Hills. By then, however, orders had come for me to report to GHQ India before proceeding to 111 Indian Infantry Bde as IO. So on 4th June 1943 I left 63 Bde for good, and in the boiling heat of the plains, made tracks for GHQ India.

3
Chindits
111 Indian Infantry Brigade

I reported to GHQ and was sent in to see the Intelligence people, who told me where I was going and what I was expected to do. A lot of mud has been slung at GHQ(I) and I have no doubt they have their faults, but the people I had to deal with I always found helpful and efficient, and in subsequent dealings, of which I had quite a few, I had no reason to revise this opinion. I saw Maj.-Gen. Crawthorn, the DMI, who was extremely pleasant, though ever so slightly ruffled when I told him I hadn't been to the 'I' School at Karachi, and above all things wanted to avoid going. I wasn't quite as blunt as that, but he got the gist of my remarks all right.

On 14th June I arrived at 111 Bde, who were then at Ghatera, in the Jubbulpore area in tented camps, and reported to my old and new brigadier- Lentaigne, and his Brigade Major, John Masters, now Lt.-Col. and DSO, OBE, a very fine soldier and a very good friend of mine. Without exception in this war, I, as Bde IO have been older than all my Bde Majors, but Jack Masters was the most glaring example of all. I found I was nine years older than he was.

The brigade staff was complete, except for one... the missing man was the Brigade Intelligence Officer.

Two days later a captain in the Burma Rifles entered my office tent. His clothes were covered in mud and he had a ragged, long-jawed face, lined, pale and sweating profusely. He saluted and said in a harsh, slightly nasal voice with the faintest touch of London on the accent - "Good morning. I'm Hedley. Where's the manager?"

"The manager?"

"The Bara Sahib. The Big Cheese. The Boss."

"The Brigadier is out," I said coldly. "I'm the Brigade Major. What do you want?"

My visitor divested himself of a rifle with fixed bayonet, a pack that must have weighed seventy pounds, a heavy haversack, equipment with full ammunition pouches and several grenades, a couple of huge knives, a dah, a kukri, a revolver, revolver ammunition, binoculars, compass, map case, a waterproof portfolio and a large sack. His khaki shirt was black with sweat. "I'm the Intelligence Officer of this crowd," he said. "The manager got me out of 63 Brigade. Here I am."

John's intelligence, determination and unorthodox mind were to be of immense value to all of us. (John Masters)

The brigade, when Lentaigne first arrived, consisted of 1st Bn. Cameronians and 4/9th GR, and they had been training since early April. We were to get the 3/4th GR in July, and much later, in September, the 2nd Bn. KORR (King's Own). So by the end we were a big force for a brigade.

Ghatera had purposely been selected as a suitable site because it was far from any towns, Ghatera itself being a small mud village on the railway between Saugor and Jubbulpore. It was in jungle of sorts but neither the hills nor the jungle were as big as Burma, which was a pity. I am fairly well used to heat, but the heat at Ghatera - usually round the 115° mark - was the worst I ever remember, and undoubtedly took a lot out of the troops.

The second Chindit show, no doubt for reasons which were unavoidable, suffered considerably from 'snowballing.' Our Bde, which began training in April, was due to go in in October. But not only did *it* get added to but more brigades got added, and then they started putting off our D Day - so much so that after a time we thought we were never going in. We did finally go in in March 1944, which meant that two, at any rate, of our battalions had been in training, much of it in very trying conditions, for a year. This was far too long, and by then they were both stale and a bit tired.

Training at Ghatera wouldn't have been very hard but for the fearful heat. As Bde IO I had all the usual routine stuff, plus lectures on the Japanese Army,[1] but I had not yet got an Intelligence Section of my own to train, and really had not enough work to do. I therefore asked

---

1   I gave these so many times during my army career that towards the end had considerable difficulty in staying awake during my own lectures.

to be allowed to train the defence platoon, and this was received with great delight by the management. The Defence Platoon were Gurkhas, and were grand fun. I greatly enjoyed my time with them.

During the whole of this time we were plagued by GHQ officers. We were the showpiece of India - though, of course, tremendously secret - and any GHQ officer who could make out he had been 'called in for consultations' by us could swing a tremendous line. I don't think we ever had the Field Bakery Section or the Mobile Bath Unit, but that's about all we didn't have. Lentaigne and Masters were both working about 15 hours a day, and these visitors were an awful nuisance.

We moved from Ghatera about the middle of July, and combined our move to Jubbulpore with a scheme. Luckily the rains had broken by then, so it was a good deal cooler, if somewhat damp. We took about five days over the move and then spent a week in Jubbulpore in a sea of mud on the rifle range and making out indents and drawing equipment. The Bde was then to do another scheme going back to Saugor, but as I had been sent up to get some intelligence information from GHQ, I only joined the scheme at the end. We spent a day in Saugor, and then marched north to a place called Gona, where we stayed in another sea of mud for five or six weeks - in a tented camp. As a matter of fact I enjoyed Gona. It was pleasant country, the rain had cooled things down a lot and apart from the routine Intelligence lectures and one or two courses, which I ran, I was chiefly engaged on musketry with the defence platoon. We did a lot of firing, and I then had to supervise the grenade throwing of the whole Bde HQ, some 100 strong. I managed to get through without anyone handing me back a fizzing grenade and calling for Mother, and in many ways that was the best fun of all. The Bde Signals Officer, a sturdy Yorkshireman of the name of Briggs, was of the opinion that safety lay in distance and threw the thing such a hell of a way that we hardly heard it explode.

We left Gona at the end of September and did another six days scheme to fetch up at Dukwan, our final place of training. Dukwan is some 25 miles from Jhansi, and there is a large dam there. The dammed up lake has several inlets, and these provided excellent places for practising river crossings, which is what we were there for, primarily at any rate. Special Force HQ by this time had been established at Gwalior, half way between Jhansi and Delhi. We did a few schemes, but not large ones. We had another blanketing as, in spite of anti-malarial precautions, few had avoided malaria at some time or another during training, and were also filled up with extra rations, vitamin tablets etc. This, combined with a very pleasant cold weather, bucked us up enormously. I don't think in all my time in the army I have been in a happier mess than Dukwan, or one in which I have had more real good hearty laughs. We were a large mess, and had quite a lot of visitors too. One of our best additions was Lieut. W.O.Lucas of the USAAF. He was a grand fellow and we all liked him. As we were to have USAAF support we needed a Liaison Officer and we were lucky in Bill Lucas. Blunt, cheerful, hearty and intelligent, he did excellent work in fostering co-operation.

As I have already stated, our training consisted largely of river crossing. I have the greatest admiration and respect for Johnnie Gurkha, and admire his manifold qualities, but swimming is not one of those qualities, as he is very poor at it. He is as willing as you could want, but he can't swim. Our other pupil, the mule, differed somewhat from Johnnie. I have the greatest affection and respect for the mule, and admire HIS manifold qualities, and one of these IS swimming, at which he is very good. Where he differs is that he is NOT willing. So our job was to overcome Johnnie's inability to swim, and the mules' unwillingness.

We had certainly taken on something! Looking back on it, our real trouble was that we tried too many methods, and I don't think really had the right one even at the end. I shall remember the fights we had with those mules for a long time. At exercise they were hard to beat, and few things have given me such a sense of satisfaction as being beaten two or three times by a mule and getting him over the third or fourth time. We tried every imaginable device, rafts, inflatable lilos, swimming, Mae Wests and, though I've been through so much training in this war that I'm sick of the very word, I think I enjoyed that part more than any other during the whole war. I think my affection and admiration for the mule really dates from Dukwan.

One rather pleasant interlude was a visit to the West African Brigade, which was training some 40 miles away. They had only just arrived in India and asked for someone to give them some idea of Burma. I stayed with them three nights and handed out nine lectures, which left me pretty dry by the end. They were a good lot of blokes, and I much enjoyed my short stay with them.

We had Christmas and the Christmas celebrations at Dukwan, and soon after that the whole Bde was ordered to move East. At last we were to see some action. Being Bde IO has advantages at times, and one is that when the Brigadier moves you go with him and not with the Brigade. So, instead of toiling across India by train, we two went up by road to Gwalior, spent a couple of days there, and then flew to Comilla with Wingate and the various planning heads, i.e. brigade commanders, BGS etc. Comilla was 14th Army HQ, and we were there to find out what our job was to be and what the Army was going to do, etc. This, of course, didn't concern me very closely; I had to get all the intelligence information I could from Army. This chiefly consisted of road information, but as we soon found my maps were far more up to date than theirs were, instead of me copying their maps, they copied mine.

During December, I was sent to Imphal to get the latest Intelligence and road information from 4 Corps. This was a pleasant trip, and gave me a chance of seeing many of my old friends.

We spent a week in Comilla, a pleasant place as they go in East Bengal, and then flew over to Imphal. Lentaigne knew by then what our job was to be - to go in by foot, and his job, with me lending what assistance I could, was to decide where we were to go in. Force HQ by this time had been established some six miles north of Imphal, and using that as a base, we visited, by jeep, a number of places, in order to pick the brains of the people on the spot. We started off at 4 Corps, where we met our old friends, then went south to Tiddim, where our old Div, 17th, and old Bde - 63, were in position on Kennedy Peak and were battering away at the Jap positions on Mile 52 without any success. From there we did a 200 mile drive back to our old haunts in Kohima, where we stayed with Charles Pawsey, and finally returned to Force HQ in Imphal to write the report. Lentaigne decided that the only feasible place was where the Chindits went in first time, i.e. in the region of Sittang, but by then it had been decided we were going in by air: so we might have saved ourselves the trouble. I don't like to think what would have happened if we had tried to go in overland, as we should have met the Japanese coming to attack Imphal head on, down narrow tracks, and there would, I know, have been some confusion.

During this time the Brigade had come up by train to Silchar, and was marching through the hills south and west of Imphal, so as not to give the show away by marching or lorrying up the main road. After they had arrived, we went into a camp in the jungle at Mile 31 on the Tiddim road, and just waited - more waiting! We had one or two odds and ends to clear up, such as ground co-operation with the L1 and L5 light aircraft which were to be used for evacuation of casualties from forward airfields, dropping maps, etc., issuing of maps, or final checks on men's documents, but apart from that we really did very little.

One of the things we were doing was searching for possible landing grounds. This was done from the air, and so many recces were made that after a time Wingate said all recces were to include some offensive action so as not to arouse suspicion. I went in a Mitchell, and as I was the bloke chiefly concerned - we were looking for water that day - Col. Cochran, the USAAF commander, very kindly put me in the co-pilot's seat. I had a superb view, and then, having done our recce, the time came for some offensive action! We selected Wuntho. We dropped one bomb, fired all 10 of our .5" machine-guns, and fired two rounds out of our 75mm cannon - for one afternoon I thought I had had my money's worth!

Once more we were getting into the frame of mind in which we thought we were never going, particularly as it was by then early March with only two months to go before the monsoon. However, having just made up our minds we were not going, Special Force telephoned us at 10 pm one night to say we were to be at Tulihal airfield - 23 miles away, by 7 am the following morning. The Brigadier had been to dinner with the 3/4th GR, and came back full of good cheer and wassail. Never one who minds a row when he knows he is in the right, he got on to Special Force on the blower, and did he tear them off a strip? It was a first class example of really bad staff work, and he told them so in terms which could be heard all over our camp! He then had Lt.-Gen. Scoones, the Corps Commander, out of bed, and he gave us one entire GPT Company: so we had part of the Brigade on the airfield by 10 am, and the rest the following morning.

This was it - no doubt whatsoever this time. We knew that we were going in to Chowhringee, the airfield in the jungle some ten miles south-east of the junction of the Shweii and Irrawaddy. From there we were to cross the Irrawaddy back to the west bank and then start cutting the railway between Wuntho and Indaw. There were two jungle airfields further north and on the west of the Irrawaddy, but these were not enough to accommodate the whole number of troops to be flown in: particularly when it was found that there were logs on one of them and it was unusable. So only two jungle airfields were to be used, one east and one west of the Irrawaddy, the one east of the Irrawaddy having been picked at the last moment when the logs were seen on the one west of the river. This meant that instead of going in fairly close together, Bde HQ and the two Gurkha Bns. were to go in with us, and the two British Bns. were to go in Broadway (west of River) and we were to join up later. At the last moment it was decided that one battalion, the 4/9th GR would land with us, but then go east and harass the Bhamo road: so we were to be left with one battalion only. Each battalion was organised into two columns of about 400 men each.

The fly-in started on 5th March, the first to go, of course, being the gliders, to prepare the airfields for the Dakotas which were to bring in the bulk of the troops. It was a good sight seeing them going in the moonlight. Until they had established the airfields, of course, we could not move. Having gone full bat for Tulihal we had then to wait a few days there! There are many stories told about the gliders, one of which broke adrift over a lot of paddy fields, made a perfect landing, not even the glider, let alone the personnel, being damaged. With great presence of mind the crew set fire to the glider, repulsed an attack by an enemy patrol, and then, seeing a large enemy HQ advanced with a view to attacking it. Luckily they heard some people talking English, and so did not attack 4 Corps HQ, which they were going to do, having landed just outside Imphal.

Despite some casualties and crashes, the gliders succeeded in their task of building the airfields, and the fly-in proper began. Not all, or even the larger part of the fly-in was taking place from Tulihal. There were also troops being flown in from Hailikandi, which is in the Silchar plain - much further to the west.

Tulihal was then a strip of no less than 4,000 yards length - reputedly then the longest in the world, and was made from paddy fields. In the dry weather, therefore, it was an excellent strip, though dusty. The organisation of that fly-in was a masterpiece, and went absolutely like clockwork. Everyone had been told off by plane-loads, and there was an officer i/c pretty well every aircraft. I had two mules, one horse, their three drivers, and a further nine men - mostly my intelligence section, in addition to myself. We all, of course, had our arms and equipment. We had our dinner, slept, were woken in time to get ready, and then were called to the control tent by loudspeaker. They checked us, and gave us two cans of drinking water, there being none in our area. Then we had to march up the runway to our aircraft. The aircraft at the side of the runway were turning their engines over, and every four minutes one of the laden Dakotas went roaring down the runway. Curiously the mules and the horse didn't mind that, but just as I thought we were safe, the aircraft behind which we were marching revved its fans up full blast, and we found ourselves in a sandstorm. However, even this only set the mules and the horse back for a moment or two, and we reached our aircraft without further fuss or bother.

Each aircraft had been stripped inside except for cross bars which had been fitted in front for tying the animals: and we also had coir matting down. We were given 45 minutes to load. There was a ramp up to the door. Mule No.1, with its driver pulling and the rest of us on a rope behind its haunches went in, and we tied its head up. Ditto mule No.2. The horse then went in all right, but the mules weren't for being squeezed out - there only just being enough room for three. Also, I suspect professional jealousy entered in. However, after a five minutes barging match we got them in, lashed bamboos across their haunches, and there we were, ready in 15 minutes. Was I relieved? Dakotas were leaving every four minutes throughout the night, and, more wonderfully still, arriving and leaving the jungle airfield at four minute intervals at the other end.

The bravest men at Tulihal that night, I think, was the Wing Commander. As Dakotas were going off every four minutes, and as there was no wind, the dust wouldn't settle, and pilots couldn't see to take off. So he got in his jeep, and his adjutant in the back with a strong lamp. When a Dakota wanted to take off, he got in front of it, and drove like the hammers of hell down the runway (he could see well enough) with his adjutant flashing the lamp at the following Dakota, which bore down on them like a great monster and took off over their heads! He was never quite caught.

We got a perfect take off, and were soon well up, to climb the hills. It was a full moon, a perfect night, and the countryside below looked marvellously peaceful and quiet. There were, of course, almost continuous jungle fires. Had the Japanese had any idea of what we were doing, or of flying at night, we'd have been absolutely dead meat to night fighters, as we went singly and had no escort. But not one Jap aircraft came up. We got to the airfield in surprisingly short time, and a remarkable sight it was - huge arc lights along the runway, hung in the middle of enemy occupied territory, and aircraft, with their headlights on, coming in to land. We circled round once or twice until we got the green from the Aldis lamp on the ground, and then down we went, with a perfect landing, and at 2 am on the morning of March 9th 1944, I once more set foot in Burma. It was a great feeling. We unloaded the aircraft, thanked the pilot and crew, and departed to dig slit trenches.

To go in detail into all the places we visited on the Chindit campaign, would be wearisome and not particularly interesting - so I shall stick to the main episodes. The 4/9th GR - 49 and 94 columns - moved off to the Bhamo road, Langford (BBTCL) being their eyes and ears, and we marched to the Irrawaddy, which we were going to cross just below Inywa. There is a large sandbank there, and that reduces the channel to about half a mile. We were going to get a special glider drop of heavy stores for river crossing - e.g. ranger boats with outboard engines etc. and gliders, having floats as well as wheels, prefer sand to anything else to land on, we had the perfect landing ground 20 yards from the water. Over they came, with a brilliant moon, no obstructions, and a flare path laid out for them. The nearest landed half mile away and the furthest one-and-a-half miles. So instead of having a 50 yards carry we had a half to one-and-a-half miles carry. That wasted about four hours, plus two extra as they had turned up late. We had already made up a raft on which we had placed 22 mules, and at about 1 am they started off, being towed by ranger boats. The engines kept on stopping, and it took four-and-a-half hours to get over, and then it was one-and-a-half miles downstream: so there wasn't a hope of getting the raft back.

Meanwhile, I had had the job of tying up four traitor police we'd captured and putting them in a glider with the American pilots. I then witnessed what is quite a common thing with gliders, but looks most eerie, particularly at night - a glider being 'snatched off.' The glider puts its towrope in a triangle on two long poles in front of it - see sketch, and the towing Dakota swoops down with its towchain with a hook on it and snatches the glider off without landing. The strain is

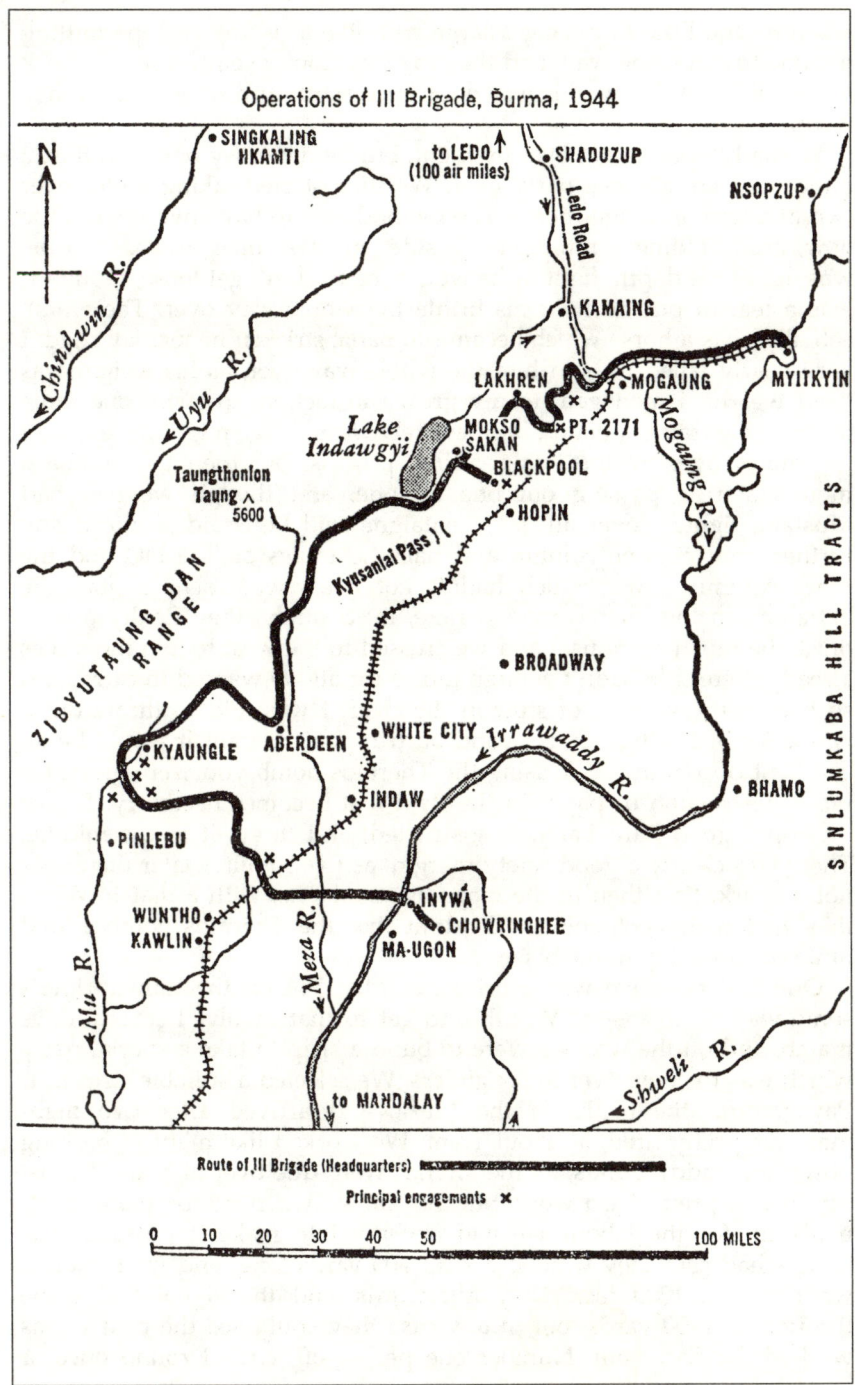

Operations of III Brigade, Burma, 1944

taken by the Dakota having a large reel, like a fishing reel, permitting the line to run some way, and they say you don't even feel much shock in the glider. Anyway, this was quite successful third time, and off they went.

We had hoped to get over by night, but by dawn we only had the 22 mules and an advance party over. We then started taking mules over two at a time in ranger boats. The method was to have two men in the bow, each holding a mule on one side, and two men drove. Once he was out of his depth, fight as he would, he couldn't get loose, though it was a fearful pull to hold his bridle the whole way over. The worst, actually, was a horse which became so panic stricken he just lay rigid. I very nearly failed to hold him the whole way over, as his weight was dead weight. I managed, to my great satisfaction, to swim one mule over; so my training hadn't been entirely wasted! We might have got all the mules over by the two-at-a-time process, but then the outboard motors started passing out one by one, and though we had had Mustang fighter cover all day, Lentaigne said he couldn't afford any further time. So one column and half the mules of Bde HQ and the other column (those which hadn't got over) were sent to join the battalion on the Bhamo road (where, incidentally, they finally turned out to be much more use) and we crossed to the west to join the mules already there. We hadn't enough mules for all we wanted to carry, and so had to throw a lot of stuff in the river. I was told to throw out a whole lot of intelligence gear and burn it, and thought it would be an excellent opportunity for using the Thermos bomb you were given for rapid destruction of paper in the field if it becomes necessary. I gave the top a good hard bang, as instructed, and threw it in the middle. There was clearly a good safety margin, as five minutes later there was not a spark. So I then lit the maps as usual - i.e. with a match. When they had really got going, I'll admit that the Thermos bomb added quite considerably to the blaze.

Our first objective was a bridge at Mile 554 on the railway line - some way north-east of Wuntho; to get to that involved several days march, and on the way we were to build a strip to take a special party which was to come over in six gliders. We selected a suitable strip near Payagon on the banks of the Meza, and arrived after two night marches, pretty tired, at about 1 am. We worked like maniacs bashing down the paddy bunds, as the aircraft were due over at 5 am. I must say, it was pretty hard work, but the 'show,' when it took place, quite made up for the labour we had expended to make it possible. The gliders had said they wanted a strip 400 yards long, and we signalled we had one 1200 feet. They afterwards said the signal had come through as 1200 yards, but in any case they could see the runway, as we had the flares out. Number one peeled off, circled round once or twice, and came down (they landed at 60 mph) ten yards from the far end of the runway, and with the most fearful rending noise charged into the jungle - in which a platoon of Gurkhas were sleeping, having been told not to. I have never seen Gurkhas break cover faster. Within two seconds of landing it was invisible from any direction from more than five yards. The last, and most drum splitting crash, which had ripped a wing off left no doubt in my mind as to what state we were going to find the occupants. We all ran to the spot - I hoping the man next to me could run faster than I could - to discover one man had cut his thumb.

Pilot number two had obviously been doing some quick thinking. He wasn't going to be such a fool as to land at the far end of the runway, not he. So he landed 100 yards short of where the runway began. Bund number one smashed his wheels and bund number two smashed his floats - splat! It took 60 of us 20 minutes to shift it out of the way, but anyway nobody was hurt.

Number three had obviously done some quick thinking too and was a man to profit by the mistakes of others. Having seen one land too long and the other too short, he obviously came to the conclusion that they were landing the wrong way altogether, and he came down at exactly 90 degrees to the runway. The procedure was by then fairly standard: bund number one accounted for the wheels and bund number two saw the floats off - splat! We didn't even worry to go and see if anyone was hurt that time.

Numbers four and five landed well, but just as number six was about to cast off we had a fine example of an officer exercising his initiative. Though it was no business of his, he considered it would be dangerous for the next one to come down for a few moments, so to warn the glider he fired off the red verey pistol (after all, what else is it for?). This, apparently, was the signal for "Enemy have taken the strip." So the last glider went home.

They really are the most terrifying things, those gliders. They make no noise bar a swooshing sound, come at 60 mph and can turn far faster than you can run; while experience made it abundantly clear that being off the runway was no guarantee of safety.

During all this time we were getting drops every five days (and very welcome they were), always at night, and I wish to pay my tribute to the pilots and crews of Transport Command. We had chiefly RAF, who were superb, though the USAAF were also good but lacked the RAF's knowledge of the country. But for the skill and daring of Transport Command, who never failed to find us, we should indeed have been in Queer Street. It may be as well, now I am on the subject, to mention the work of the USAAF under Col. Cochran. They gave us tactical support in Mitchells and Mustangs, in which they were first class, but even more did we have occasion to thank them for the way they flew out our sick and wounded. We built a number of airstrips, in paddy fields, often, inevitably, in most difficult places. They made some remarkable landings and take-offs, and many of our sick and wounded would have had to have been left in villages but for their skill and daring.

After bringing in these gliders we moved off for our first objective, the bridge at Mile 554. For pretty well the whole of our first three weeks we were marching, and routine was roughly as follows: Up before dawn and stand-to; cook tea and eat your K ration breakfast. March until 12 o'clock, having probably started at 7 am, with halts of 15 minutes per hour. Rest from 12 to 3 including lunch. March from 3 to 5.30. Get into camp, stand-to, cook after dark (tea only), eat your supper and sleep. Much the hardest part of all was the marching, as you knew that every step you took, uphill and down dale, you had that ghastly burden on your back.

My work as Bde IO consisted of keeping up the situation maps, sending and receiving reports by signal, and generally finding out what was going on from such locals we captured, in co-operation with Macpherson (BBTCL) our Burma Rifles officer, and Smith (Port Trust) our Burma Intelligence Corps officer. When we built airfields for light planes, I sent off road and track reports. And then we all took a turn as orderly officer during the night and deciphered any messages which came in.

We got the bridge all right, and with a glorious bang the central span disappeared 40 feet into the Nga-Ne Chaung. I afterwards heard the Japs had trains going over it ten days later, having spanned the gap with a bridge built of wood. There is no doubt the Japanese were the most remarkable engineers, and their ability to improvise was quite amazing.

After that, we were ordered over onto the Pinlebu-Mansi road in order to harass it. This involved some very hard marching over the Mangin range north of Wuntho and the path was not made any better by rain. However, we got there, none of us any the worse for wear. The day after we had blown the bridge, however, we received news that Wingate had been killed, and that Lentaigne was to fly out to take over the division. This involved building another strip, which we did, and saw our new general fly out, while the BM, Jack Masters, took over.

We put down a series of small roadblocks, picking off a few Jap lorries, and getting quite a decent score of stiff Samurai, but there was no question of putting down a big permanent block, though we were by now a force of five columns, having joined up with 41 and 46 (the two King's Own columns) and 26 and 90 (the two Cameronian columns). It was somewhat galling in Bde HQ. One's job in HQ, as was impressed on me, was to direct, not to fight, and I know that to be quite right, but it was none the less galling for all that, not to be allowed to go with the ambush parties.

After we had been doing this for some time we moved off once more, crossed the road to the west, and moved into the upper headwaters of the Chaunggyi Chaung.

We stayed here some time, harassing the roads round about, and also managed to clear the Japs out of a village called Nyaungwun, which was a fairly big dump. We got a good number of documents from there and then burnt the whole place to the ground, a task made easier by the Japs having conveniently left 2000 gallons of petrol there as well as everything else. I must say that the best thing to see go up was case after case of men's personal belongings. Having lost all my stuff I was quite content to see a few hundred Japs lose theirs.

After that, while the Bde was more or less stationary for a bit, I was sent off on a long recce. The USAAF said they had bust the road leading west from Thyetkon over the Zibin Taungdan, at a place some four miles west of the range, but this was to be confirmed by ground recce. I took my orderly, Kundal Gurung, as staunch and faithful a Gurkha as one could ever want to meet, two RAF sergeants and three privates from another brigade altogether, but who had been put in the wrong aircraft when we came in in the first place. So we were an assorted collection. Those who have worked in Chaunggyi will know that the Zibin Taungdan is a very sharp escarpment, and there are very few ways up it. The ridge two miles to the east and parallel to it is scarcely better, the two together being rather like two giant railway lines. The country between is very largely uninhabited, and as a result game abounds.

> ...John Hedley was sent off on an independent mission with a handful of troops... It was an unenviable job involving some very strenuous marching and no fun at the other end. John called up his troops... and briefed them. He would never do anything by halves and went into the minutest details, instructing the men to carry toggle ropes and gym shoes for the climb, also a plentiful supply of salt. There was something rather scout-masterish about him in his brimming enthusiasm and we chided him, but he was quite impervious to ridicule answering back with one of his rich, throaty laughs. He disappeared into the jungle with his long raking strides so that his men found some difficulty in keeping up. (Richard Rhodes James)

We started off up the Nantagun Chaung, a sandy and very pleasant chaung that cuts through the first ridge. The problem remained of finding the way up the escarpment. This, however, proved easy, as we found the track - still marked as clear as day - which the refugees had made when they came out that way, and their camping and cooking sites were also clearly visible. We got up the escarpment, and I meant to get to the road that night, but by thoroughly bad map reading got onto the wrong track. We got there the following day, hitting the road some two miles east of the place where the road was supposed to be breached. We lay up until dark, and at 11 pm I was going to walk up the road with one of the RAF sergeants and have a look. Luckily it was a dark night, the moon not being due to rise until 3.30 am. I wasn't in much doubt as to whether the road was breached even before I started, as, as soon as it was dark, lorry after lorry started passing us from the direction in which the road was supposed to be breached. As they were all filled with empty petrol drums they made a noise one could hear miles off. We started off at 11.30 pm and made one-and-a-half miles before I decided to leave the sergeant, as his boots were making too much noise. The whole way we had to keep jumping into the ditch as lorry after lorry went past us. I went on at least another two miles, and so was well past the spot where the road was supposed to be breached, and was just going to turn back when I saw a lorry, heavily camouflaged, at the side of the road. It was so heavily camouflaged that I couldn't see which was bow and stern. I flashed my torch to see what was inside and heard a sleepy voice talking a language which by a process of exhaustion I took to be Japanese. Not being sure where it came from, I made the lorry a present of a grenade and moved off to a safe distance. I came back hoping to find the situation in hand, but found that all that had happened was the grenade had landed in the body of the lorry and had merely succeeded in waking the driver up. By then I could see which was the cab, and a lucky shot through the door gave me my one confirmed Samurai.

Having got my information, we started back, but owing to some of the worst map reading that even I have ever done, took one-and-a-half days longer than we need have done. After one of my longest and most inexcusable 'diversions' I really felt so ashamed that I apologised to the party. Private Ryan, of Liverpool, with a face exactly like the standard caricature of a prize fighter, answered "Oh! That's all right Sir. We'd just eat all our — khana and then lie down and - well die." They really are wonderful fellows, the British Tommies.

John Hedley, pale and sweat-stained as always, swung into camp with huge strides at the head of six of the most exhausted looking men I have ever seen. He was carrying three of their rifles as well as his own. I offered him a tot of rum but he refused - he had sworn not to take a drink until he was back in Mandalay, having driven out the Japanese who, in 1941, had driven out him and his family. Taking off the pack, the equipment, the rifles (it was exactly like his first arrival at Ghatera), he gave his report.

The country across which he had travelled was *perfectly bloody.* Gorges, cliffs, mountains and dense forest, much of it spiny bamboo, whose spines, sharp as needles and hard as steel, are three to ten inches long. The second evening he took up position beside the disputed road, and saw trucks moving cautiously and wide spaced along it. The RAF were wrong, and his job was done. But that was not enough for J.D.H.Hedley. In the middle of the night he walked along the road with his orderly, felt the surface and noted what it was made of, what damage had been done by bombing, where and how it had been repaired, and what signs he saw of damage to trucks. During this walk he found a truck stopped, the driver asleep in the cab. Having shot the man dead, John catalogued the contents of the truck, and only then set out to rejoin us. (John Masters)

...He, John Hedley, had killed a Jap. He regaled us with details and his fierceness was a bit frightening. The victim had been in a parked lorry, sitting at the wheel; John Hedley lobbed in a grenade and followed up with the bayonet. Lo! the spoils. John, ever the good intelligence officer, laid before us a badge of rank and an identity disc. (Richard Rhodes James)

When we got back, we were told the Bde's task had been radically altered and we were to put down a road and rail block just north of Hopin. This involved 17 days almost continuous marching, and was much the hardest bit of the campaign, as there was some hard and steep going, and the weather - it was now well into April - was getting hot. We marched through the Namsaung forest, skirted Mansi two miles to the east, and stayed the first night between Naungpat and Namsayeik, and there we had our 'concert.' This needs some explaining. One of the absolutely fundamental principles of jungle warfare is silence, and one of the most trying things is never being able to raise your voice.

So, if you're sure there are no enemy anywhere about, it's a wonderful relief for troops to be able to let off steam. As there was also an issue of rum that night, it was a disturbed evening, as everyone was allowed to sing as much as he wanted all night - and many did.

We then turned south-east through the Kalat R.F. to Manhton, on the Meza river, a pretty spot where Aberdeen, the Dakota strip, was situated, protected by one or two battalions of West African troops. It was to this field that casualties were brought by light planes, to be ferried from there, by Dakota, to hospitals in India. we stayed a day there, and then started off up the Meza. We slogged up the bed of the river for two days. In its upper reaches it has no valley at all, jungle covered hills rising steeply on both sides. We then turned east, tramped over some extremely pleasant hills, inhabited by some extremely pleasant Kachins, and finally descended into the Indawgwyi Lake area. The lake is, I think, one of the loveliest spots Alvei seen in Burma. In the rains, of course, large areas round about the lake flood, but in the hot weather this is covered by long high grass, much of it being sword grass, which will cut like a razor if you're not careful.

We spent a few days here, waiting for the rest of the Bde to concentrate, our camp being at Mokso Sakan, about half way up the lake on the east side. From Mokso Sakan we marched over the hills to our east, and established a fortress on a hill a mile west of Namkwin village. It took us three days to get there, and was the most fearful going I ever remember, and was made worse by rain. How some of those mules went, with loads, up some of the places we got up I just do not know. After my time with the Chindits, I will never again say a word against that superb animal, even though he seems (to the uninitiated) sometimes 'to move in an mysterious way his wonders to perform.' No other animal or machine could have given us the help and service which those mules did.

Our prize mule was the mighty Maggie. Of prodigious strength, she was nevertheless as calm as could be wished, and only twice was she ever known to misbehave. Once was when we emplaned, and nothing would make her go in. The other was when some GHQ officers came down to look at our mules. Maggie, of course, was picked out as our star, and celebrated the occasion by catching one of the GHQ officers a royal punt up the bottom. But we were never able to decide whether that was the worst thing Maggie ever did or the best. She was hit and one of her legs nearly blown off in a bombardment, but she just went on calmly grazing until we shot her. She was a real character and a wonderful animal, and there were many more like her.

The fortress was a hill some miles from the road and rail, and below us was a Dakota strip, which we had built. The first few days consisted of having stores flown in, digging trenches, wiring etc. We were to hold that block against the Japanese to prevent large numbers of them getting north to the relief of Mogaung and Myitkyina, both of which places were tottering. Our position was pretty strong, particularly when we had 25-pdrs flown in, but, of course, it was not across the road and railway, and I put this to Jack Masters and asked if I could go out for a night to observe the road and railway. He agreed, and told me to take Sgt Pullen, of the Cameronians. I should add that the previous night the Japs had tried a small attack, but had been driven back with casualties.

Before going out, we had been told that the main line bridge had been bombed and was thought to be completely wrecked, but that the Japs had built a small loopline. Our orders were to look at the two bridges, then go on and see what the road bridge was like and also observe what was going up the road. We started at dark, creeping down the bed of the chaung, which was about six inches to a foot deep, and keeping, of course, well to the side. We got to the first crossing, the diversion, and as that was thought to be undamaged I felt sure there would be a patrol there, and crept up to it with extreme caution. However, either there was no guard there, or else we were so quiet that they never heard us, for we were not troubled, and were able to examine the diversion at leisure. The Japs had been remarkably neat about it. The chaung there was about 50 yards wide and they had built an embankment out 23 yards from each side: so there was only a 12 foot gap in the middle which could be spanned easily by two girders. Of course, when the chaung came down in spate, it couldn't get through a 12 foot gap, and would wash the whole embankment away: but why not, it was only for the cold and hot weathers, so the Japs hoped. To improve matters, they had put sand over the top so that an airman taking a quick look might well think it was a road.

We moved on from there, the next port of call being the main bridge. When 40 yards off we could see it had been the recipient of at least two direct hits, and was very sorry for itself. We moved on cautiously, and had just got up into the embankment to cross, when a Samurai bolted out from under the bridge, threw a grenade at us as he went, and ran down to the bottom of the embankment to wake his fellows: I fired automatically and as automatically missed, and then took a look round to see who had fired the shot, failing to observe the presence of a fizzing grenade five feet from me. However, I received notification four seconds later, when it exploded. It was enough to knock me over, and to push a small splinter into my right knee. Pullen was unhurt. And that demonstrates what in my opinion is one of the greatest advantages we had over the Japs in the war - weapons. All our weapons were superior to the Japanese counterpart, and in no weapon was this more marked than the grenade. A British grenade at five feet would have blown us both to pieces. I know of two more blokes in our brigade who had a Jap grenade explode five feet from them, and neither of them were hurt.

By this time I'd collected my wits somewhat, and both Pullen and I threw grenades which landed - and exploded, exactly where that sentry was jabbering to his section commander: so I have high hopes we bagged a few more that time, but can't put in a definite claim. We had hopped back over the line to be out of the blast of our own grenades.

We lay up for ten minutes, and then crossed the line 100 yards lower down. We got to the road, not at the road bridge, but as we could hear lorries driving down into the chaung and up the other side, were justified in assuming that the bridge was broken. We observed for five hours, saw 500 Jap troops going north, and got back without further incident except that by then my leg was getting a bit stiff.

The doctor examined my leg. It could hardly have been a smaller wound, but the knee was very swollen, and as the doctor thought the swelling would not go down until the offending particle had been removed, I was ordered out. I was due to go out on 10th, after dark, from our own airfield. I must say, I didn't think I was going to get off. In the middle of the strip, but on one side, was a Dakota being repaired. The Japs started shelling it from long range with a 105mm gun. After about 15 shots they hit it. They then started ranging on the far end of the airfield, where the aircraft had to get to take off, the airfield being as short as it could be consistent with being a Dakota strip. After about 20 shots they had obviously got their range, and stopped: clearly to shoot up aircraft trying to take off. A bit later down came our Dakota - and not a spit from them: so we took off as easy as winking. They are the most odd people. We landed to pick up more wounded at Broadway; so I got out to be able to say I'd set foot on four of the five aerodromes, and three hours later I was in hospital in Sylhet.

That was a first class hospital, and I was in a week, after which the swelling went down, and it was not necessary to dig the splinter out. I'd only been in two days when in came my old friend Patrick Boyle, who had taken over Bde IO from me. He had been sitting in my trench, doing my job, at a time when I would normally had been there, and a shell splinter hit plumb on the crown of the head. Nobody will tell me it wasn't meant for me. I'm glad to say the splinter just hadn't penetrated far enough to do permanent damage.

After I got out I was convalescent for a few days and then, as I was not allowed to go back in again, I was sent off on my 31 days war leave. I went first to Dehra Dun, to pick up my kit. Normally I never expect to see kit again after putting it in any army dump, but this was an exception. Not only was it all there, but all the clothes had been dhobied! I went up to Simla for my leave, and before the end of it received orders to report to Delhi, having been transferred to Force 136.

So ended my time with the Chindits. I am glad I had that experience. I won't say I didn't have too large a proportion of training for the amount of action we subsequently saw, and I wish I'd been on the first as well as the second show. But that is about the limit of my criticism. On the long credit side, first must come the feeling that after all the years of waiting, we were at last doing something that was of real value to the war effort. Second, I suppose, comes the number of lifelong friendships I made, particularly Lentaigne to whom, incidentally, I owe pretty well all of such knowledge of jungle fighting as I possess. Finally, there was the interest of the whole show, the places one went to, scenery one saw, and the opportunities one got of realising what a grand and interesting country Burma is. Yes, I'm glad I was a Chindit.

4

Force 136
Operation BISON

...It was perhaps as much due to Hedley as to anyone that the XIV Army was no longer expressing criticism at the lack of intelligence reports from the clandestines. On the contrary there was a signal of praise for the reports being filed...[1]

W hen we were at Imphal, on one of the occasions when I thought that even after getting that far we were never going in, I had applied to go to SOE[2] (Special Operations Executive). Lentaigne had refused, but said he would send me after the campaign, and he was as good as his word. Incidentally, I should have seen no more of the war if I had stayed in the Chindits as, owing to a number of factors, they finally fizzled out and took no part in the final advance on Burma. So, on 14th July 1944, I reported to Delhi, was promoted to major as from that date, and after a few days spent in various preliminaries, went down to Calcutta. I discovered my CO was an old friend of mine, Lt.-Col. R.G.Gardiner GM of Macgregors, and as good a man as one could want to work for. He told me he wanted me to raise and train a number of groups of natives of Burma, with British officers, capable of operating in small groups behind the enemy lines. This struck me as being the answer to all my dreams. He then handed me over to his GII, an old Burma man, but who had not got that dynamic grasp of realities so necessary for a staff officer. He didn't last long.

He told me that he had been up to the refugee camps in Assam (it will be recalled that when the Japs broke into the Imphal plain the villagers from the Kabaw valley were evacuated) and had picked out a perfectly superb lot of fellows: "Complete lot of cut-throats, old boy, and probably can't read or write, any of them, but wonderful material -

1   Terence O'Brien, *The Moonlight War: The Story of Clandestine Operations in South-East Asia, 1944-45.*

2   Force 136 was the SOE organisation in Burma charged with running intelligence agents behind Japanese lines, liaising with friendly tribes, sending back information. Their agents also, at times, inflicting damage and/or casualties.

only need training." As I'd been told our first job was likely to be a series of co-ordinated attacks on Jap airfields to destroy aircraft on the ground - a job for which you've got to be prepared to accept 100% casualties if necessary, I was glad to hear I had got something pretty tough! We were to go to Poona, where we had a filter and training school, and the GII said he'd send me a directive later.

The men arrived - 24 of them. They were a decent lot of simple villagers; only two had ever walked 15 miles in a day in his life - and that minus any load, one was blind in one eye, one was the typical fat flabby village headman - aged 56 and a dear old boy, and one had a permanently dislocated hip from the age of seven! The only one who had ever fired a rifle before, I discovered subsequently, was a deserter from a similar organisation. We moved off to Poona, where we had the filter course. This is a most interesting type of course, consisting of a series of practical tests, mostly team ones, which soon give you an idea who has got leadership and initiative. In the middle of the course, the directive arrived and I remember it included these words:

"You will bear in mind that the men under your command will be better able to perform the tasks allotted to them if they are able:-

(1) To march 30 miles a day for three days on end over jungle tracks.

(2) To carry a pack of 50lbs.

(3) To drink once every 24 hours."

I replied that they would be even better able to perform the tasks allotted to them if they were able:-

(1) To march 1,000 miles a day for a year over glaciers.

(2) To carry a pack of one ton.

(3) To drink once a month.

They had as much chance. All but four of them failed to pass the filter and those that did only got through on regrading. So we scratched the fixture and started all over again.

The next few months were a bit of a nightmare, and there were occasions when I thought we were never going to get things organised. We got officers fairly soon, and though one or two dropped out for various reasons, most of them lasted and did useful work. The men, however, proved a stumbling block, as the only personnel any use for this type of job were Burma Riflemen, and they were up in Dehra Dun, under command of Lt.-Col. P.C. Buchanan, MC late BBTCL. About four different organisations were putting in demands for these men and the Chindits, under Joe Lentaigne naturally weren't parting until they knew what their own future was going to be. High level conferences, in which GHQ(I), ALFSEA, SEAC, Burma Army and about four other hangers on took part, and conference after conference shelved the question in, I consider - and ask Peter Buchanan if you don't believe me - a most disgraceful manner. Consequently it was not until September that we got any men to train.

That wasn't the only snag. Distance was another. We had our main HQ in Meerut, Administrative HQ in Delhi, Operational HQ in Calcutta, training schools in Poona and Horona (just outside Colombo) while the parachute school was in Rawal Pindi. So it covered practically the whole Indian Empire. As we were super secret, all mail had to go by safe hand, which meant it sometimes took a fortnight and had missed the man concerned when it arrived, and delays were many and inevitable. Before the men arrived, I was busied largely with HQ work, getting out training directives, and generally doing what I could. I also went up with a whole mob of officers and we did our first parachute course.

Parachuting is the greatest thrill I know, and I wouldn't have missed it for any money anyone could offer me. The course only lasts five days, and really there's very little to it. You start off on the swings, i.e. you get upon a high platform in a hangar, put on your harness and jump off. You are, of course, attached by long wires to the ceiling. This is to practise the take-off, which is far more important than the landing, as nine fatal accidents out of ten take place as a result of take-off being bad initially. On the swings you do your turns, correction of spins, etc. Then for rolls, falls, slides down chutes to practise your landing etc., but the thing you get sickest of is the jumping drill. You get into these mock-up fuselages and jump out into a sandpit one after another. You do it over and over and over again till you get sick and tired of it: but they're absolutely right. Nothing is more important than correct drill going out: in fact almost the only way you normally have a fatal accident is by two blokes, owing to bad drill, going out together and getting tangled up. That and gremlins.

I cannot over-emphasise that gremlins should be treated with the greatest respect. In parachuting, which is always low level, we do not meet spandules, which take over from gremlins at 10,000 feet, but that would be no reason for not treating spandules also with respect, even though one is bound to feel a somewhat distant reserve. I had only heard tell of four of the gremlins stratagems, and am thankful to say they have never yet considered me a worthwhile objective. One type of gremlin waits till you are airborne and then runs round the canopy gnawing through the shroud lines till the canopy comes loose. Another carries a large wooden hammer. He goes out with you, and while you are looking to correct twists, slowly turns your quick release button and then gives it one good clout with his mallet, causing you to drop out of your harness. Another, in need of relaxation, gathers his friends together, and they all dance together on the top of your canopy until it collapses. The last is not, repeat not, airborne. He walks about under aircraft from which men are parachuting, and under his arm he carries the worst piece of ground imaginable, normally an almost precipitous rocky bank with a bed of cactus at the bottom. Down you go - perfect take off, beautiful position, knees and ankles together, elbows in, shoulders rounded, watching the soft green field you're about to fall into. But he's watching you too, and just as you're about to get the most perfect roll you've ever had, he pulls out the green field and slips in the really dirty piece of ground instead.

There's not a man living who does not have just that bit of fear when he goes out, or rather just before he goes out, but parachuting has one great advantage over, say, a bayonet charge: you can't change your mind and go back. You've only got to make up your mind once. I went No. 1 in my first jump, and got a good take-off. I've only been out of Dakotas, and the first thing you are conscious of is wind, as at the moment you go out you are in the blast of the port propeller's slipstream. This turns you to the left, and you then have the sensation of slipping down a grassy bank as you lie back on the slipstream. Then suddenly: dead calm, as you drop under the slipstream. You then adjust your twists, if any, stop any oscillation, take up your position and wait until you land. I got a back landing the first time, but made one or two mistakes. One was to have my head well back, another was to have my mouth open and the other was to have my tongue out. My feet hit the ground first, then the back of my head - skipping my bottom altogether. The result was that when we did the second jump the day after I had slight concussion, and had only a very hazy idea of when I was going to hit the ground. But that time all was well. As there was a thunderstorm we failed to do our night jump, and so were not considered as having qualified on the course.

Once the Burma Riflemen had been obtained from Dehra Dun, the authorities having at last made up their minds, training started, but to start off with I was supervising. This involved almost endless travelling as Rawal Pindi could never take more than two groups at a time; so there were groups all over the place and I've seldom moved about quite so much. I know nearly every main line in India as a result of those few months. However, things got better when the Meerut HQ moved to Kandy, the school at Horna for musketry, demolitions etc. was enlarged and we ceased to use the RAF parachute school at Rawal Pindi, having set up our own at Jessore, some 80 miles from Calcutta. I went down to watch two of our groups in the jungles south of Belgaum, and from there went straight to Colombo by train and ferry. I arrived at Colombo station at 9 am and by 11 am was in hospital with malaria - a good start. However, when I got out my troubles were largely over, as all I had to do was to hand over the groups to the extremely able control of the OC School. He was Lt.-Col. R.Musgrave, late of the BBTCL up country, and a better man it would have been hard to find. It didn't take him long to pull the whole show together and get it working really well.

We had Christmas there, and did a whole lot of last minute jobs, and also had some extremely pleasant trips down to the sea. There is some of the best bathing in Ceylon one could ever wish for.

Meanwhile I had taken over my group which, after one or two changes, finally consisted of myself in command, Captain Nimmo 2 i/c, Captain Marchant, Captain Buchanan, Sgt. French, Sgt. Romain, Sgt. Cottingham (W/T operator) and 16 Kachins or, to be more exact 15 Kachins and one Karen who had got mixed up with the Kachins.

We were roughly briefed as to what we were going to do, and on January 14th 1945 flew up to Jessore from Ceylon, with just one stop at Madras. There was a smallpox scare on arrival so we were vaccinated almost as soon as we stepped out of the aircraft.

Operation BISON

When there are a large number of operations of similar nature taking place simultaneously they are all given code names, which are in a series, i.e. all flowers or all fish etc. In this case we were an animal series. Operation BISON was the operation for which we were selected. We were to fly in, in two Dakotas, at 45 minute intervals, and drop on a DZ (dropping zone) some three miles south of Baw, which is a village some ten miles south of Maymyo. Our tasks were:

(1) To establish W/T communication with base.

(2) To observe the road and rail between Maymyo and Mandalay.

(3) To indicate suitable bombing targets for the RAF.

(4) To harass the road and rail but only when so ordered.

(5) To prevent the Japs destroying certain specified objectives, but again, only to do this as and when ordered.

As we had been trained, amongst other things, in ambush and demolitions, we all hoped we would get some of tasks 4 and 5, but the orders never arrived and we had to be content with 1, 2 and 3.

We had a week in which to make absolutely final arrangements, work out detailed plans, decide who was going in which aircraft etc. and on 22nd January, 1945, at 5.30 pm we took off from Jessore, and I shall have to live to be a pretty old man before I forget that night. I was in the first aircraft with Marchant, Romain and nine Kachins, and the other was to follow 45 minutes later. We were to bring them in onto our DZ with torches. Well, off we went, some of us singing, some sleeping, some reading - as long as it was light - all trying to make out we weren't scared stiff when we knew damned well we were. It got dark quite soon, and after a bit the despatchers said "We're over the Chin hills." I tried to picture in my mind's eye about where we were. A bit later they said "We're over the Chindwin" and once again I tried to calculate where we were. All this time, the despatchers (two of them) were heartiness itself - why shouldn't they be - they hadn't got to go out. After a bit, I thought it about time they put on our sky-hooks, but they seemed quite satisfied to leave it a bit longer. (The parachutes had been fitted before we emplaned, but we were not wearing them, and particularly in the dark, and with all one's equipment they are not too easy to get on.)

When we were, I estimated, about level with Shwebo, they started to put our parachutes on. Despatcher No.1 was first class, despatcher No.2 was a novice. So the procedure was that despatcher No.1 put on No.1 parachute then took off the parachute which despatcher No.2 had put on our No.2, readjusted it, put it on again and then went to No.3, and so on.

By the time we were over the Irrawaddy there were still five to put on, and a bit later, when there were two left, the pilot came to the back of the aircraft and said "We're due over the DZ in five minutes, why the devil aren't these parachutes on?" and tore the despatchers off a good long, broad strip. The despatchers assured him all would be ready by the DZ: so the pilot went back to drive his aircraft. The last two, however, proved particularly obdurate, and by the time they were on we had already made three runs over the target, with reds and greens for jumping coming on like Saturday night at Piccadilly Circus. Having made his dropping runs, the pilot came to the back once more, to make sure the only occupants were the despatchers, and was somewhat ruffled to find the status quo unaltered. A longer and even broader strip came off the despatchers. However, they assured him that all the parachutes were now on, and there could be no further trouble: so the pilot went back once more to drive his aircraft.

And then the door stuck. They kicked it: they pulled it: they turned the levers up, they turned the levers down; they kept a running flow of the most horrible abuse I've ever heard: but the door knew all the answers, and we made three more runs over the DZ. Well, you see, when you're going down blind on a DZ ten miles from an enemy Army HQ, it doesn't assist security to make six dummy runs over the target. The pilot, just to make absolutely certain nothing could possibly have gone wrong this time, paid us another visit and, of course, tore the despatchers off the strip of the century: and then the despatchers started putting their case to the pilot in vigorous parlance. You can imagine the confusion: dim purple light, everyone talking and blokes tripping over the packages which were going out after us. It would not be an over-statement to say that at that moment my morale was low.

Well the pilot had had his say and after a bit went back to do some more driving. By this time they got the door open and had hooked up the first six of us. I was No.3 in the first stick. Well, I have never refused to go out yet, but I really think if I'd been No.1 I'd have said to the despatcher: "Go and ask the navigator to check the course." Because I could see we weren't in the right place: there were rivers and ravines and jungles below us in profusion, but little else. However, I was No.3: so two had gone out before me: but the real reason was that I thought if the pilot came to the back of the aircraft once more, it would be safer outside than in!

So out we went. The best take-off I've ever had, no twists, and practically no oscillation in the calm cool night air. I don't ever remember experiencing quite such a pleasant sensation. First of all there was the thrill of knowing that after months of wearisome training we were really started: then there was the heartening spectacle of seeing those six parachutes in the best line I've ever seen. We must have had a perfect take-off, as you could have put a ruler along the line, and we'd all have been on it and all at absolutely regular intervals. But finally there was that feeling I've only experienced when parachuting at night - the feeling of being, for the first time, almost apart from the world spiritually as well as physically. The natural scenery, also, with the hills and ravines bathed in moonlight, were of great beauty, and I had a feeling of wonderful peace - for a bit.

I was only able to permit myself a few moments of soliloquy, as that was not what I was there for, and I started to study the ground for the DZ. However, my suspicions that we were in the wrong place were soon confirmed, for as far as the eye could see there were hills, jungle and river: so I knew sooner or later it was the trees for Hedley. Down we went: and down: and down: and still more down. I began to wish I'd brought a book. However, at last I reached ground level, but as I reached it about midway between the tops of two hills, continued on my way unimpeded by any firm obstacle for another 1000 feet, while the hills rose on all sides. However, parachuting for me is very much like riding a horse, in one respect, viz it is only a question of time before I hit the ground. I saw I was going into a tree, and debated whether to do the drill or not. This consists of doubling up your legs to cover your stomach and putting your hands across your face. That's all right if you are going to hang up. But if, by chance, you get through, or if, as may be the case, the tree is only some ten feet high your bottom will be the first thing to hit the ground and your spine will go flying through the top of your hat. I decided not to do it. A branch caught me across the upper lip, missing both my nose and my teeth: a moment of blackout and I was swinging gently from the top of the tree. It took me two minutes to pull myself from the trunk and slither down it, and then, according to drill, we put on our torches. The aircraft made three more runs and we heard slight noises from time to time as personnel and packages came into contact with timber, and then silence.

Johnnie Marchant was, curiously enough, only ten yards from me, but where the rest were, or the packages, I had no idea. Clearly the first thing which I had to do was to get up the hill and try and find the DZ and off we went with that end in view. But it was quite useless, as also was the attempt to find the other men or the packages: so we lay down and went to sleep. The other aircraft having gone to the correct DZ, of course, never found us and returned to base.

The day after I found the rest of the party and all the packages except the wireless set. None of the party was hurt except myself, and I only split the inside of my upper lip, the result of not putting my hands in front of my face as I should have done.

And now I am going to digress - on the subject of DZ's - for, though it may surprise the reader, the RAF's error in navigation was not only one of the chief factors in the success of the operation, but also taught me one of the most important principles of this type of operation - that you should not go in on a 'proper' DZ. This may strike the reader as so much horse-radish, but let me explain. A parachute force of the Arnhem type goes in with the object of fighting a really fierce battle the moment they touch ground - probably having heavy casualties and being overrun by the main army after, at most, three or four days. So they must get onto the ground in as near perfect formation as possible. The company commander must know, on landing, that if he faces the way he has come from, say, his CSM will be the first parachutist he sees, that his mortar team will be in one bunch on the left etc. and it's no use having a mortar team if the barrel is stuck up a tree and a large number of restive Nazis are moving towards them. So for that type of operation a perfect DZ is essential because the quintessence of the whole scheme is speed.

With an SOE party these conditions do not obtain at all. Your objective will seldom be less than a week, and may be as much as three months ahead of you, and the very last thing you want to do is to start a rough-house, as the enemy, if he finds you, will always be able to bring absolutely overwhelming forces against you. What you want, therefore, is not speed, but secrecy. Your battle is half won if you have got in without anyone knowing, and it doesn't matter if you take three days to find your party. You have masses of time. Now the number of paddy fields and taungyas in Burma is legion, but even so, they are the places near which the Japs will have warned the villagers: they are the places near which an odd villager may find your containers and put the Japs on your trail: and they are the places which may be staked and panjied. But to watch all the jungles of Burma is a task before which the imagination boggles. So if you can get down in jungle - unhurt - your chances of a secret entry are, I consider cent per cent. Now can you? The book says "No," or at best "doubtful." But I am absolutely sure you can go down - barring freaks like landing on HT cables - in anything except a high wind. According to the 'book' (all ranks should stand to attention and salute, whenever the 'book' is mentioned), we couldn't have landed in a worse place - very steep, the ground largely rocky, and completely covered in thick jungle. Yet my split lip was the only casualty, and that was my fault. Sgt. Romain, after getting down, did 20 feet on his bottom down a rock face, but was quite unhurt. Furthermore, there is no doubt in my mind that there is a sixth sense which watches over a man in danger.

In training, you know that if you break a leg, stretcher bearers and ambulance drivers will have you in hospital in five minutes, where you will be nursed back to health by a bevy of dazzling blondes, I don't say you will try and break a leg - even for such a prize - but you'll know subconsciously there's no permanent danger if you do. But if you know that if you break a leg you're going to spend three months in the jungle with a bamboo splint tied on with parachute cord, well, somehow you won't break your legs: And the fact remains that there are far fewer accidents in action than in training. So if ever again I take in a parachute special force, there'll be no selection of DZ's for us.

So much for that digression. The next day, by carefully plotting where the packages which we had found had fallen, we gauged where the lost ones must be, and found them after a three hours search. While they were being taken back to our camp, I took a havildar and decided to go on until I found out where we were. You see, it isn't so easy as it sounds. Nobody knows more about getting lost owing to bad map reading than I do, but whenever that has happened, I've always known where I've started from. But we had started from Jessore, and might not even have been on the right map, and hills look very much alike. However, after a long tramp I saw one river with a huge loop in it - it was unmistakable on the map, and I was able to identify our position. We were just north-east of the junction of the Namtu river and the Yegyan Chaung, in the BBTCL Pyoungshoo forest, and were, therefore, the wrong side of the Namtu, being 14 air miles too far South. I got back to camp to find the wireless set, when turned on had emitted a column of black smoke. a large dent in the side of the set - where it had landed, explained the sorry position. The wireless set was US.

We had arranged before we went in that if anything went wrong we would go to the DZ south of Baw and an aircraft would search for us on the night of the 28th. So the only thing to do was to move off north, and, if possible, get to the DZ without being seen. We started off up the east bank of the Namtu on the 25th, but eventually arrived at a small village called Ngata Sakan, and had to get boats to cross. We spent the night with the villagers, and the following day managed to slip away before dawn and gave the villagers no clue as to where we were going. We still had plenty of time to waste, and did so by lying up in the jungle.

On the 28th a Dakota came over and found us, and gave us a drop of more food and, much more important still, two new wireless sets, both of which were undamaged. Our wireless operator was on the second aircraft, and so had not yet come in: but Johnnie Marchant and I could both operate the set, we managed to get our message through, and on the night of 31st January we brought the second aircraft in onto the DZ with torches, and the rest of the party baled out in good order and landed in good order.

To get to our objective we had to get right down into the Lema Chaung and up the other side: and as staying where we were was just asking for trouble, we beat it on 1st February. A large amount of stores had come in with the party, and I don't ever remember tottering under such a fearful load as we carried that day. We were all carrying at least 80lbs, including arms, and even going, as we were, downhill, we were all exhausted at the end. Even so, I had to send a party back the following day to bring the balance, and this they did successfully. We had established our first camp, one mile up the Ngapwe Chaung, which is the name of the upper reaches of the Lema Chaung.

Our next job was to get in the 'cache' drop. This needs a bit of explaining. When you go in on a show like this, one of the first things you must do is to get away from your DZ. That is obvious, and to do that you must go in fairly light, as you can't carry a great number of stores when you have to carry them all on your backs. When you have moved to a spot you consider suitable for a cache, they send you a Liberator and he gives you a big load - a month's supply of food, explosives, steam generators for recharging your wireless batteries, extra clothes, a Bren gun and other spare arms etc. so that you have a decent sized base. Now the RAF to start off with said they could only drop when there was at least half a moon (later on they dropped on pitch black nights) and that being so, we had to get the drop in the next two nights, or wait a fortnight. The original idea had been to get across the chaung and up onto the plateau before taking the cache drop, but that scheme had been knocked endways by the second half of the party not getting in until 31st January. So I asked for the drop in the bed of the chaung, but said I didn't want the heavy stuff like the explosives. Dropping aircraft, of course, must keep at least 500 feet above hill top, not ground level, but are prepared to do high level dropping in, say, a deep ravine, if the ravine is straight enough to give them a reasonable chance of finding it.

We got no reply, but were expecting them on 3rd February, and with that end in view built some fine bonfires in the bed of the chaung. The following day, I took two men and we went off up the hill to try and find a suitable camp site on the plateau, as to get to the road from our camp in the chaung would take one day each way. So I handed over to Bill Nimmo and went off. We found the site we wanted, and nearly got back in the day but had to sleep on the hilltop. During the night I was woken by a most beautiful and melodious sound - to my ears at any rate - to wit the droning of the engines of a Liberator, and it seemed to be flying down the line of the Ngapwe Chaung. There was, however, one thing that night which I did not hear - a tiger which walked within three yards of my head. My two Kachin boys, however, knew what to do about that. They didn't do anything stupid like trying to shoot him. Had they done so, they'd only have wounded him, and then we'd have a screaming maniac to contend with: no, they flashed a torch in his face, and he beat it. A tiger, presumably the same one, visited our camp twice more, and on one of these occasions again failed to wake me though only three yards away. And on both occasions the Kachins worked the torch trick on him: so it is worth remembering.

I went down on the 5th, and of course asked what the result of the drop had been. From a height of 3000 feet above the chaung bed the Liberator had put eight of the containers bung in the chaung, and the other four we found a maximum of 400 yards away. Pretty marvellous dropping, and typical of the support we got from Transport Command throughout the campaigns in Burma. They deserve far more recognition than they received. Ask any that have been supplied by them and see what they say. Liberators were far better than Dakotas, as Dakotas can only push out six packages at a time at the very most which means two runs, and in addition the packages are bound to fall in line. Liberators, however, put all the containers in their bombracks, and only carry maximum of four packages. These they can discharge in one run over the target, and as they all go with one push of the button they all come down together.

The day after, 6th, we were going to move up the hill to our new camp, but as we would not able be to carry all our stuff up the hill I had to leave a base party. We struggled up Nwalabo Taung, and then moved along the top of the ridge. we had to pass near some tangya houses: so we lay up until after dark, and got to our new camp unseen by anyone. Our old camp would soon be found, I knew, as one of the Kachins had rather excelled himself the day before. I had put him on a track some 300 yards from the camp to ensure we weren't surprised. He saw a villager, who had no suspicion that we were anywhere about, and instead of hiding and letting him pass, arrested him and marched him bung into our camp in broad daylight. I couldn't hold the man a prisoner, so had to let him go.

The following day, 7th, we got a signal asking for a road recce miles away to the east, and particularly, if there was a road running south from Kangyi and crossing the Namtu. This was clearly a case for a detached recce, and I sent Nimmo and Havildar Gum Ja Naw off for 12 days. They put up a splendid show, covered an immense amount of ground, and came back with all the information they had been sent for. I'm glad to say that for this recce and the consistently first class work which Bill did throughout operation BISON, I was able to get him a well-deserved MC. I could never have wanted a better second-in-command, and the Kachins would do anything for him.

Well, that was Bill and Gum Ja Naw off, and now for the road. I left Johnnie Marchant and Donald Buchanan to select the campsite, and took two men and went off. The jungle in this area is not thick, as jungles go, but there are some wicked slopes, and even when we found the best route it used to take us five hours each way. The first day, however, it took eleven hours. It wasn't really entirely my fault, as not knowing what new tangya villages might not have been built since the map had been printed, one had to proceed with extreme caution. We finally got up onto Kyaing Taung, which stands two miles east of the road, and which is a hill I shall always regard with the deepest affection. It gave us a grand view of the road and the approaches to it, and from it it was possible to see the best and safest way to our objective. When we moved our camp further west, it was to Kyaing Taung that we moved. It was our haven and our fortress and will be one of the first places I shall visit when I go back to Maymyo.

From Kyaing Taung there appeared to be a good approach to the road down a spur which reached the road at about Mile 32, and we went for it. Actually, we got a bit too far north and ended up in the pineapple gardens, which those who have motored up to Maymyo will remember start about Mile 32. I left my two men and went forward to spend a night at the side of the road. I was greatly disappointed to find no pineapples - being out of season, as they would have provided a very useful addition to our diet. But you can't have everything. As soon as I got to the road I discovered that cover was so good that barring incredibly bad luck or pure carelessness on our part there should be absolutely no difficulty in observing the road night after night from a range of, at most, five yards. I spent the night jotting down everything which passed up and down the road, and by 1 pm was back in our camp - very tired - with our first contribution since the operation began. It was a great moment, even though there had been no pronounced troop movement one way or the other.

> After the drop [Hedley] and his team of four Burmese established themselves in a hide just ten yards from the side of the main Mandalay-Maymo road and from there the reports he filed of Japanese traffic were of such staggering detail as to mark a sudden appreciation by the XIV Army of the value of Force 136 agents behind the lines in Burma.
>
> Hedley did not merely report the number of trucks that used the road on any one night; he attempted tto give details of each particular truck in the convoy, its tonnage, its contents, the enemy unit associated with it, and anything else that his senses could detect or his intelligence deduce. His passion for detail was renowned. (Terence O'Brien)

Thereafter, for the next ten or 12 days, the procedure was more or less standard. The road patrol, consisting of one officer, one NCO (British or Kachin) and two Kachin Riflemen went off at about 11 am, got to the road just before dusk, observed the whole night, left the road about 5 am (the Japs never used the road after that time and it gave us half an hour of complete darkness in which to make sure of our escape) and by 11 am the patrol was back in the camp. The reports were then made up and enciphered, and soon after that were being deciphered in Calcutta. Our means of communication was with the B2 set, as beautiful a set as ever one could see: packed in two watertight metal boxes, each of which weighed only about 20 lbs and powered by a six-volt wet cell accumulator, it had a range of at least 2000 miles, quite possibly more, and was a real work of art. The only job was the recharging of the accumulators, and I should think orders on this subject covered half of all the orders I gave on the operation. We first of all tried a hand generator which had to be clamped onto a log or any solid object, and which proved to be too weak. We thereafter relied on the steam generator. This was great fun. It consisted of a large steel furnace, in which was fitted a cylinder with a screw top, capable of standing up to high pressure. From this one or two steam pipes could be led off to a small machine which charged the accumulators. The furnace boiled the water and the steam ran the machine. The great advantage of this type of machine was that it ran on firewood so no petrol was necessary. In spite of the excellent precedent set at Kawkareik, we did not have firewood flown in, but managed to collect it ourselves. I shall always remember the evenings spent around the steam generator. We were only able to cook food before dawn or after dusk (smoke, which you cannot hide, gives you away; flame you can hide easily by day or night). So after the evening meal, if you were not on the night patrol, you used to sit around the generator, poking sticks in from time to time, while the purr of the machine indicated that the work was being done for you - always a pleasant feeling. Needless to say, we always brewed an extra cup of 'char,' and swopped stories and reminiscences till the steam had run out, when we turned in. Yes, they were very pleasant, those evenings, and we got to know each other much better than we should have done without them. Sgt French was one of our most interesting. He was, and is, a publican in peacetime, and taught me more about the ins and outs of that trade than I'd have dreamed of. I am assured of drinks at the Crown, Hatfield Peveril, near Clacton!

The system of W/T was that we had two 'skeds' a day, one of an hour and one of half an hour. the times varied with the day of the week, but at those times the air was yours. Then on top of that there was a 24 hour emergency sked, which you could call up at any time of the day or night, but were only expected to use when either you had urgent information or were in trouble. When the Japs started moving we used this sked quite a bit, but to start off with there was not much traffic, and what there was roughly balanced out each night.

During all this time the remainder of the food was being daily ferried up from the camp at the bottom of the hill, and just lasted out nicely. We couldn't have operated from the first camp in the Lema Chaung, as the patrol would have been too long, and we couldn't go to a forward camp at Kyaing Taung at this time as, had we done so, we would never have been able to get the food up. The compromise solution was the only possible one.

We only regularly watched the road by night, as it was only by night the Japs moved in any numbers. On two or three occasions we did do complete day observations as well (the cover was so good that we were able to observe even by day from 15 yards range) but there was no movement so I decided it was not worth the extra sweat and risk.

The railway line was some two miles away and I did once send

Johnnie down to the line for a night. He saw what trains were going. But for the rest we used to listen for the trains and report so many up and down per night, and the management were quite satisfied with that information.

The only sort of excitement during this time was on returning from patrol one day. East of Kyaing Taung there is a track running north-south, and on it one day we ran into two locals. After talking to them for a moment I realised they were spies of the Japanese, one an Indian and the other a Shan. I was a fool. I should have opened fire on the spot, but asked them a question or two and at that moment some village women came round the corner. Not wishing to be seen by them we got under cover and the spies bolted through the women and escaped. It was entirely my fault. However, I reflected that it would be six hours before they could get to Maymyo, and by then, so far as they knew, we might have gone 15 miles in any direction. It would clearly be useless for the Japs to come and look for us, and I reckoned the most they could possibly hope to do would be to put a patrol on the track and warn villagers around to be on the lookout for us. So I gave orders for great caution to be exercised when crossing the track, and also with regard to villagers. Anyway, apparently it was effective, as when we eventually fell back on Maymyo, I asked the villagers and they said they had never been warned by the Japs. It is my belief that during the whole time we were in operation the Japs never knew there were British troops in the area. Towards the end, I thought it would be more sporting if we offered the Japanese a handicap, but the management would not hear of it.

Nothing much of importance moved until February 14th, and then, in addition to the ordinary traffic a whole lorried battalion went down, and from then on until Maymyo was taken there was a constant stream of Japanese troops down the road. There were some marching troops, some animals, but most of the troops and all of the stores went down in lorries, which always came down in the early part of the night and returned from Mandalay in the second half of the night. The most important thing, of course, was to record the information accurately, but one could do quite a lot by making some deductions. One night three lorries went down, one with the fuselage of an aircraft in it, and two more with one wing each. As, however, there had been 13 other lorries in convoy with these, and they contained stores and personnel, it was highly probable that the ground staff of Kangyigon aerodrome was on the move, which we suggested to the management.

There was never any difficulty in getting off the road, but getting onto the road was more difficult as the Japs, knowing the RAF would not, for choice, land in the dark, used to bag the last half hour of dusk for movement, and frequently sent down their most important troops then. Once or twice it was quite tricky getting onto the road unseen; I remember one evening very clearly. We had got to within about 600 yards of the road, and were just preparing to make the last jump, when two Mosquitos arrived on the scene and went into action without any further ado. Now, I'm all in favour of getting into a good OP at the side of the road, but not while two mosquitos are spraying the road from a height of 50 feet with cannon shells. So we waited till the fireworks were over and then started to move down. We had not got far when I heard a lorry coming. We hurried up, not wishing to miss anything, and it occurred to me it was making a lot of noise, even for one of the passed out old rattletraps which the Japs were using: and then the truth dawned on me - TANKS. Of course, if you're an intelligence party, tanks are the 'pearl of great price.' As if by instinct, the whole party broke into a mad rush, and what would have happened if we had met the Japs I don't know - except that they probably would have been the most surprised men in Burma when they saw us. Anyway, our luck was in: we met neither Japs nor villagers, and saw ten of them go past. They were the only tanks we saw, and as that was the only occasion aircraft strafed the road I've a pretty good idea we had an agent in Maymyo who had tipped them off. But, of course, we are quite rightly not allowed to know anything about any other parties. Men who get caught behind the Jap lines get boiling water poured up their noses till they give away all the information they know: so the less they know the better.

That evening contained another most illustrative incident. Being February, it was pretty cold at night, and in addition to plenty of warm clothes we used to take one or two lightweight blankets. On one occasion a cart stopped opposite to us, a Japanese army cart, and the Japs fell out for a drink. I thought I'd have a look and see what was on it, and walked up. I had my blanket over my head, like one used to see villagers when the poor devils had any. I was just getting fairly close when one of the Japs walked up from the other side. We were about three yards apart. I couldn't have missed him but we'd have only started a lot of unpleasantness, would have had to have left the road that night, and they might have started searching for us. Also, we had been told our job was intelligence and action was to be avoided at all costs. On the other hand, I thought, this man will surely think I am a villager so I walked away. He was quite satisfied and did likewise. Now, you see you could never get away with that in the front line. If you are on patrol between the two front lines the enemy will always be expecting to see you. But in our position we always had the element of surprise, and one of the most important things for a commander of a party of this nature is to convince his troops what enormous advantages they have over the enemy, excepting only that if he finds you he can bring overwhelming force against you, you have almost every advantage. And the 'if' should be so big as hardly to give the enemy even an outside chance.

February 19th was the end of the non-dropping period, and we were due for a Liberator that night. So on the 18th we moved from our camp to the east of Kyaing Taung to a new camp right in under its eastern face. This was the best campsite I could imagine. Kyaing Taung, like every other hill in Burma, has, of course, spurs running off it, but one of these spurs had a rightangle bend in it, thus protecting us from view on all four sides (see sketch).

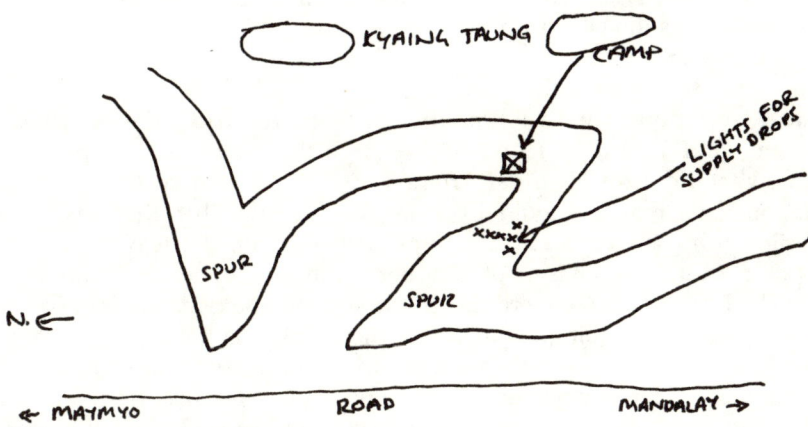

It was a perfect spot, but of course no lights in that hollow could possibly be seen from the SD aircraft, and when you are a small party, it makes a tremendous difference having your supplies dropped bung on top on top of you. A fully loaded container weighs just on 300lbs, and though you open it and take out the contents, the difference between carrying the contents of 14 containers 50 yards or 500 yards over bad ground is about a days work. So we told the aircraft we would put our lights on the top of the spur, but asked him to fly north and drop level with our lights but 200 yards to the right. The Liberators dropped to us three times at that spot, but I was only present once and it was the most perfect piece of flying I have ever seen. We picked him up with our torches when he was about eight miles away. He turned away and shot-up the road - the correct cover drill - and then flew high across our position from west to east. Another very big turning circle and he came high over our position from south to north. He turned again, but this time the opposite way, did a circle which took him well the other side of the road, came up from south to north again, but this time in a dive, and I could almost feel him coming at us - engines throttled back sparks from his exhausts and then, as he was right over us, a roar as he opened his engines up to full throttle and off he went; and five seconds later I looked round and outlined against the sky I saw a cluster of 16 parachutes all in a circle with centre the camp and radius at most 50 yards. He had only once been low over our position, and all three of his turning circles - six miles diameter at the best of times - had been different ones. No man, however acute, could have guessed within five miles where the parachutes were being dropped even if he had known that that particular aircraft had been a SD aircraft. It was the best drop I had ever seen.

But I have digressed somewhat. The move went off according to plan, and to my and the party's great joy, Bill Nimmo arrived back exactly on time. By this time the road patrol had become almost routine, and I thought to try and enlarge the scope of our operation somewhat I'd take Havildar Hpau Dau Tang round to the north of Maymyo, so that we could find out for sure whether the Japs were coming from Maymyo only or from further north. Bill was more than capable of taking charge of the party, and only he or I could be detached recces, as we were the only two who spoke native languages. It was quite hard going, as there are plenty of hills there, even though they are small. We went through the Maymyo rides, both coming and going and so can, I suppose, claim to have been the first troops in the Maymyo area. We managed to get two complete nights on the road, and also met a couple of locals who gave us some information. One was U Nu, of Letse village at Mile 47, and one was an ex-schoolboy of the SPG school in Mandalay, who spoke perfect English. We arrived back on the 26th, having been up for two nights running and then done 22 miles uphill and down dale in one day. I slept well that night.

Meanwhile, the road patrols had continued as per routine, but I thought it would be as well to move our camp, for security reasons. We had already made one dump about a mile away, and the more camps you can have the better. In jungle country, particularly where, as was the case with us, the country was also hilly, a camp even a mile away would be quite hopeless to try and find. So, if you have several camps, and are attacked, you don't stay and fight it out - you'll always be outnumbered - you just scatter and reassemble at whichever of the other camps is the agreed RV. This time we moved about three miles south, and three miles in that country would be equivalent of 30 in England.

Soon after this the management asked for another detached recce, this time to Kyaukse, or rather to the road between Kyaukse and

Mandalay. As Bill had done a 12 days recce, I felt I should go, and, taking two men, did so. We failed. We got across the Namtu, got around the hills on the other side, but then got hopelessly caught up in some very thick bamboo which was completely waterless. We struggled on for a bit, but then I gave it up as a bad job, came back and made suitable apologies to the management.

It was fearfully galling, of course, to see all those Japs going past and be unable to do anything about them. It was also maddening to hear those trains going up and down the line and be debarred from wrecking them, which we had been trained to do. It was all the more so in view of the fact that there are certain ways in which you can ambush Japanese parties on the road without committing your own party to any unpleasantness. One way is to get a whole lot of grenades, remove the works, and run a strand of cordtex through the whole lot. Run off a piece of instantaneous fuse with a pull switch on the end of that, and one man, hiding behind a rock can explode the whole lot at once. Lay the line of grenades in the bushes beside the road and if you blow them as marching troops are going past, you'll have a good chance of bagging the whole lot. Another is to sit upon a bank on the hill section, where the lorries would have to go slowly. Lob half a dozen grenades into a lorry full of troops, and let them share them. You would not, of course, do this anywhere near your own OP's, but would detach a party and send them 10/15 miles up or down the road. We were so champing about this that I had actually enciphered a message asking to be allowed to take offensive action, when a message arrived saying the management expected that when the battle of Mandalay finished there would be numbers of Jap troops pouring up the road to Maymyo, and our job would be to harass them, but that for the moment the management only wanted information. So I never sent my message. No Japs ever did come back up the road: so we were done out of our ambushes - a great pity.

We had two more shifts of camp, arriving back in our real main camp about March 10th. We had another drop there, and were really stocked up over everything. Life had become routine, with regular patrols, regular meals, regular sleep, and even regular times to listen in to the news.

On 12th we went down on to the road, determined to shoot up the first Jap we saw to get an identity. But we were foiled even in that. It was the first night the road had been a complete blank. I felt then that something was up: so took Sgt. Romain and one Kachin and pushed off to Zibingyi on the railway line where, after taking the usual precautions, we walked into the village, to be accorded a sort of civic reception by the entire population. They cooked us a first class meal, gave us all the information they could and we went back. On the way I met two Burmans who told me the British had marched through the hills and taken Maymyo. Our job on the road was over. I stupidly didn't keep a tally of what we counted, but roughly we counted 13,000 troops (Johnnie Marchant and Donald Buchanan shared the record, with 1,600 troops in one night. On two nights running - near the end, 1,600 Japs pulled out in one night - quite a good haul), ten tanks, 600 animals, 50 guns and 250 lorry loads of stores - all going the same way. We had maintained continuous observation on the road for 36 consecutive nights, and at the end of that period the Japs never even knew there were British troops in the area although our OP's were never more than five yards from the road and several were one yard from the road. It just shows what you can do if you are operating in jungle country, have a good start, air supply and exercise reasonable care. The enemy really hasn't a chance. It's a shame to take it.

Before I'd got back on the 12th Bill had gone down onto the road, having got a message from the management saying we could take offensive action against any Japs seen. They went further down the road and found three samurai. They shot them up and claimed one, but they didn't come home triumphantly bearing the stiff, so they may or may not have got him. Anyway, we signalled back we'd got one.

They also gave us orders to move. We were to move to the Kyaukse area and observe the road there. This meant crossing the Namtu, and was going to involve some heavy carrying. As I knew the Japs had gone, and as I thought it would be good to show the flag, we marched as far as the nearest village, Pawaing, and had a very friendly chat with the villagers. They told me, on questioning, that the Japs had never come to warn them to look out for British troops. They knew that there were British troops about, as, on the way back from the Namtu I'd bumped into U Kin, one of local headman: but they said they had no idea where any of our camps were. I saw no reason why we should carry these blighted packs any further than was absolutely necessary: so we asked the villagers to hire us three bullock carts, which they did most willingly, and we began our triumphal march.

We started off on the 15th, and shortly before noon had reached a small village just one-and-a-half miles north of Myebon. Here there had been a suspected enemy dump, but we had recced it on the ground and had reported that it was not a dump as far as we could see. At this small village there was a charming old Buddhist priest, to whom I paid my respects and he offered me tea and bananas, which I gratefully accepted, and was astonished to see they were served on one of my old dessert plates looted from Maymyo. It would be interesting to have been able to trace the itinerary of that plate from my house to the priest's. I then, not unnaturally, made a speech to the villagers saying Maymyo had fallen, the British were back, and their troubles were at an end. It is interesting to note that their main reaction to this was to ask, "Can you guarantee that the Chinese will never come back again?" Our gallant allies as well as being, in the main, useless fighters, left behind them, by their cruelty and looting, a memory of loathing and disgust which will probably take decades to erase.

We passed on. We hadn't gone very far when down came nine Spitfires. They bombed and machine-gunned Shwegyaung, a village one-and-a-half miles to the east, and then machine-gunned the tiny village we had just left - ten minutes after I had made my speech. It was possible some half-witted penguin (RAF for ground crew or confirmed HQ man: so called because the penguin has cold feet and can't fly) had made a pig's nose about the information we had sent back about Myebon, and we had also indicated some Japs had passed through Shwegyaung two days before. But the attack on the village we had just left was indiscriminate strafing of the worst order. We went on into Myebon, where about 20 houses were burnt down, four had been killed and two more wounded. We did what we could for them, but they were both women who had been shot through the thigh bone. And what a fearful mess those poor creatures were in. One I know died soon after, and I'm afraid the other probably did too. Apart from this, of course, I had to make my apologies, as the ad hoc representative of the British Government, to the headman and villagers, and it was with deep shame that I did it. I have seldom felt so small, and the fact that nobody offered one word of remonstration, just resignation, made me feel smaller still. We sent off a really blistering signal then and there, and I was even more definite in my report which I wrote on arrival in India. It was most unfortunate, after the superb support we had had from Transport Command, to have this climax from the fighters.

We continued down through Letpangon to Lunkaung, where we stayed the night in a house - the first we had slept in since we left Jessore. U Kin, the headman I had met when we were returning from the Namtu, was the headman of both of these villages, and did us royally. He was, and I hope still is, the real old type of village headman, and a more delightful old boy I havn't met in all Burma. He is high on my calling list when I go back that way.

That evening we 'rang up' Calcutta, as usual, and got the order to stand fast pending further orders. I knew what that meant - home for BISON - and sure enough the day after we were told to report to 62 Bde in Maymyo. So we marched back over the route we had come the day before. We arrived for the evening in the small village which had been strafed, and found they had two dead, a girl and a boy moderately wounded, and a child slightly wounded. We patched them up as well as we could, and I arranged we'd take in the girl and boy to Maymyo the day after. It was the least we could do, and was little enough in all conscience, and their obvious gratitude made me feel, if possible, even more ashamed than I was already.

The day after, we moved off, with bullock carts, and plus our two patients - and then came the most dangerous part of many operations - getting back into your own lines without being shot-up. I calculated that if we debouched on the road about Mile 28 at Pyintha, we should be south of any troops coming down from Maymyo, and so would not suddenly come roaring out of the jungle on the flank of marching troops. We all took our caps off, as they could conceivably be mistaken for Jap caps, and we all sang as loud as we could. We made the road alright and then started marching towards Maymyo, Bill and me half a mile ahead, the rest plus bullock carts coming after. When we had gone about half a mile a lorry came bearing down on us. We hollered and waved and it drew up without firing. The driver, an ex-Gloucester of 63 Bde, recognised me, and the officer said they had been warned to look out for parties of Force 136: so all was well. He told me we should meet the Bde coming down the road, and this we soon afterwards did. To make things even easier the brigadier was Jumbo Morris, who had been in command of 4/9th GR in 111 Bde, so from then on, in the words of the poet Milton, "Everything opened and shut." He gave us a note to the 2nd Bn. Welch Regt, who were the garrison in Maymyo, and that evening we were their guests in Flagstaff House. They received us most hospitably, particularly their CO, Lt.-Col. B.Cowey DSO, an old Welsh centre three-quarter. It was March 17th, and to all intents and purposes operation BISON was over.

We stayed three nights in Maymyo, and during the time we were there it was most interesting to go round the place and see how it had come off: on the whole not at all badly, and all the BBTCL houses had been spared. Several of us attended the first service held in All Saint's Church since the war began, and a moving little service it was too. The Welch Regt were there in force, and being Welsh were able of course to produce a first class choir. The church was stripped inside, and nearly all of us had to sit on the floor. The Anglo-Indian community turned out in considerable numbers, and all managed to produce a smart dress - obviously the one which had been put in cold storage for just such an occasion as this. Almost the last time I had been in that church was when I was married - a slight change since then.

We were lorried down to Mandalay and told to report to 19 Div. The driver said he knew the way, and took us to within one-and-a-half miles of the fort walls. The fort had not then fallen, and as it so happened, on that day three waves, each of three Mitchells, were due to come over to bust the fort walls with 2000lb bombs. And as it happened the first wave came over just as we were there: and as it happened the first six 2000lb bombs missed the target by one-and-a-half miles and missed us by 400 yards. And as it happened we then turned round and beat it. We found the airfield north of Mandalay and were flown out as far as Imphal that day. We stayed five days there, during which I wrote my report, and, such are the coincidences of war, had breakfast on Palm Sunday with the Right Rev. The Lord Bishop of Newcastle, and on 25th March Calcutta sent over two Dakotas. Our party was swollen by 16 Chins whom we had found in Maymyo. Two were escapees from the Japs and the others were remnants of Brian Smyth's (Macgregor's) party, which had been parachuted in to the Kalaw road to do the same as we had been doing but had unfortunately been broken up, Smyth being killed. He was a very fine officer and was extremely popular with his men. We had an uneventful trip and at 9 pm on 25th March landed at Alipore airfield in Calcutta.

Operation BISON was over. It was far and away the most interesting job I was given to do in the war, and was I am told the most useful. To one who, like myself, prefers to work on his own, to be given a job of this kind and a party of this nature was perfect. I can never be sufficiently grateful to the members of my party, particularly Bill Nimmo, for their staunchness, loyalty and cheerfulness. There was a fellowship in that party that I shall remember till the end of my days. To make things even better, we had perfect weather - as one would expect at that time of year - and some truly lovely scenery. If one has to fight a war, one could hardly ask more. It was not a hard operation physically as we had no hard marches and, except when on the road patrol, could sleep as long as we liked. Our HQ gave us most efficient and unstinted support, and we had the reassurance not only of knowing this, but in the job we were given to do we had the measure of the enemy all the time. I had complete confidence in my party, not one of whom failed in any way. We would have liked to have been allowed to spring one ambush or wreck one train, but you can't have everything.

5
Force 136
Elephant Point

After operation BISON was finished it took me a few days to get reports typed, the men paid, stores and arms returned etc. in Calcutta. During this time I was informed that I had been down for one of four areas in the Karen hills, with the rank of lieutenant-colonel, but that as I had been on operation BISON at the time, the command had been given to men junior to me. They were, however, thinking of forming a fifth area still further east, and I should be getting that. In actual fact that fell through too. It would have been a grand job commanding levies and harrying the Japs, and I should have liked to have been a lt.-col., but on the other hand I should have been in until October and so could never have flown home, as I did, at the end of May on compassionate grounds. So on the whole I think it worked out for the best.

During the interval I paid a flying visit to Poona, and returned to Calcutta in the middle of April to be told I was required for a parachute landing to take place at Elephant Point, south of Rangoon. I was given full information as to the state of Japanese and patriot forces on the ground, and was told my job was to be liaison officer between the paratroopers and patriot forces. These patriot forces were organised and armed by Force 136. The army, I was informed, would want patriot forces to protect their left flank against any threat by the Japanese, should one develop. At the same time it was explained to me that this was only part of a much larger scheme, its object being to enable the invasion fleet, which was coming in as soon as we had got Elephant Point, to sail up the Rangoon River unmolested by the two 6" guns on Elephant Point.

Now, I may as well state from the start that I don't think there was much that was right about the Elephant Point show, or about the invasion by sea either, for the plain simple reason that neither should have been put on at all; they were just a very expensive waste of time and material. I believe, but I am not sure, that it had been the intention to put the show on about a month earlier, but that it had been cancelled as being unnecessary. I also believe, but again I cannot be sure, that it was suddenly decided to put the scheme on a second time as there was panic amongst the high-ups that 14th Army unaided would not get

Rangoon before the rains were well established. Anyway, it was
decided to put it on, and weight is lent to my belief that this was a
second attempt by reason of the fact that so many of the personnel of
the two Gurkha paratroop battalions had recently been sent on leave
that when we did go in they had to combine two battalions to make
one. I believe 14th Army would have got Rangoon by the rains beyond
all shadow of a doubt, and for that reason alone the sea and airborne
landings were a waste of time.

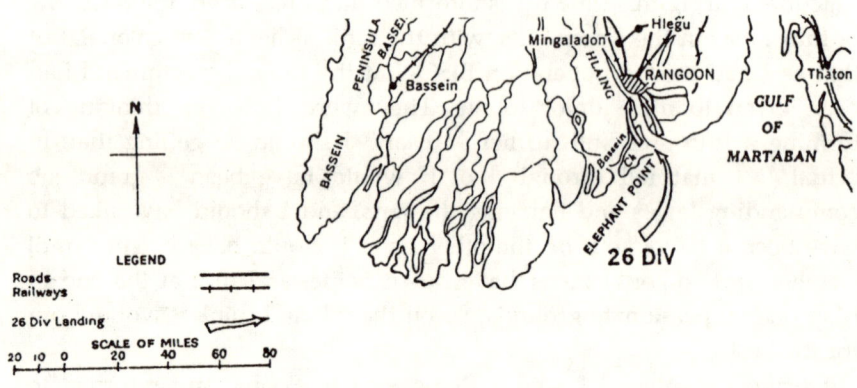

Having decided to put the two shows on, I suppose they felt they
had to go through with them. Before we went in, moreover, Force 136
on the ground had told us that the Japs had evacuated Elephant Point
and that the two 6" guns there suffered from the defect, from a military
point of view, of being made of bamboo. Still the show went on. It is
my personal belief that they said "We've had a paratroop show in every
other theatre of war except SEAC and we're damned well going to say
we've had one in SEAC." It was. in fact, a "glamour boys' parade."

Getting down to slightly more detail, it was impossible to get patriot
forces to protect our left flank in the time available. We were due to go
down at 6 am and to get Elephant Point that afternoon. For obvious
security reasons it would not be safe to give advance warning of the
plan to patriot forces on the ground. All they could be told with safety
was that on May 1st they should be at a certain spot where something
would happen and they would receive appropriate orders. Now, as
Rangoon dwellers will know, the Bassein Creek, which takes off about
eight miles from Elephant Point, cuts it off altogether, making it an
island. Between Elephant Point and the Bassein Creek is little better

than mangrove (this may be overstated, but there had been early rain, and it would have been bad going with absolutely no cover whatsoever). If the Japs were already south of the Bassein Creek in any strength when we landed (which we knew they were not) they would be able to attack us before patriot forces, not knowing what was in the wind, would be able to assist us. If, on the other hand Japanese forces tried to cross the Bassein Creek after we landed, we would have captured our objective long before they would have been able to slosh their way through the mud, quite apart from the fact that they would be the answer to an airman's dreams.

However, we'd better get on with the narrative.

We were to go in on May 1st, and with that end in view I was sent off to an aerodrome some 80 miles west of Calcutta, the name of which I can't remember. It was a vast affair which had been used by the USAAF for Superfortresses, and there were two or three squadrons of Dakotas and C47's and a fair number of Thunderbolts. The personnel were all American, and the huts, which were some three-quarters of a mile from the aerodrome, had been occupied by the USAAF ground crews. Now, however, they were occupied by the troops we were to take in, the 150 and 151 Paratroop bns combined into one, plus a number of Indian sappers. The planning was done by Col. Abbott,[1] a very capable bloke who was not, however, coming in with us. The ground commander was to be Lt.-Col. Newlands MC. The officers were a pleasant lot, but had the great disadvantage that as the two battalions had been amalgamated many were not commanding their own men.

The countryside was dead flat, just like any part of Bengal, and was of course boiling hot. They had quite a decent mess and not unnaturally we discussed Burma at dinner. The ignorance of all of them, from Col. Abbott downwards, about any aspect of Burma life was all-embracing and terrifying, and I told them so in those words.

I was not the only outsider there. I had another Burman with me - name forgotten and never of much interest. He had done two jumps from aircraft, but on arrival at the aerodrome stepped off the running board of a stationary lorry, twisted his ankle and then developed 'fever.' I think he was a plain daffodil (i.e., pretty, but yellow) and I am glad he came no further. He would have been worse than useless. Then there was Sqdn. Ldr. Edward Tull, of Force 136, and a number of RAF W/T personnel who played a most important part, as will be seen. Edward Tull was ICS, in the Punjab, but resolutely refused to return to the ICS while the war was on. He was not only tough and had loads of

---

1   The huge bombing programme was, I am sure, arranged for him.

guts, but also had intelligence and imagination. We were lucky to have him.

That was the set up. I flew to Calcutta once or twice more for the latest possible information, and while I was doing that the bn. did a practice mass landing. The CO, however, rightly refused to allow any specialist personnel to take to the air.

On April 29th we took off, and after an uneventful but quite interesting flight touched down at Akyab. I thought Akyab island a pleasant spot, though none of us were allowed into the town. Being on the sea, in my opinion, makes up for anything. The whole place, needless to say, was alive with troops, vehicles and aircraft.

That afternoon a lot of us went up to 15 Corps HQ, where there was a lot of jabber and jaw, and where the chief spokesman was Maj.-Gen. Down. He was the GOC of the Parachute Div, and it was quite obvious from what he said then and on the following day - to my mind at any rate - that he was determined there should be a paratroop show. One could easily understand his point of view; there they had been, training for months and months, and not to have had any sort of show at the end would have been very galling. However, war is war, and unnecessary waste being wrong my views as above stand.

The following day we had all the details of final outfitting, adjusting parachutes etc. and then Down came and gave us a final talk, giving details of the exact timing, bombing programme and so on, ending up with the usual good wishes, with the remark that "We were making history, being the first parachute operation of this kind in SEAC." I thought "Yes, brother, and that's why we're doing it." I had paid another visit to Force 136 that day and confirmed there were no Japs left in the area. And then Edward Tull and I put our heads together.

Now it will be as well here to explain roughly what the plan was. Without going into minute details of timing, this was it:

First of all went the pathfinder aircraft containing Tull and party, self, the press representative[2] and some of the Gurkhas and their officers. We were to bale out at 6 am just south of the village of Tawkai which is itself some five miles west of Elephant Point, and if the village

---

2   I take my hat off to this bloke. He was the sub editor of the Calcutta *Statesman*, an Indian, but unfortunately I have forgotten his name. He was dressed up in major's uniform overnight. He had had no parachute ground training of any kind whatsoever, and had never been up in an aircraft until he flew with us to Akyab. We showed him roughly what to do when we were in camp, and he went out No. 1 (actually that is the easiest place to go) in the first aircraft - a good show. I don't grudge him the article he wrote in the *Statesman* on "My First Jump," he had earned it: he was a brave man and did his job well.

was clear we were to light flares at 7 am when the main armada arrived, so as to let them know the coast was clear. I had asked to be allowed to recce the village, and had been given leave, but I needn't have worried as no sooner had the first man baled out than there was a mad rush by all the villagers to get our parachutes: so we didn't have to go for the information - it came to us. Also, I had arranged to meet the Force 136 representatives there.

At 7 am the main force came in, and from there we advanced to Elephant Point. The objective was due to be taken about 2 pm.

Now, apart from the village at which we landed, there are three villages between there and Elephant Point, in order of approach Tawkalaik, Thaunggon and Ywathitkon. This last village extends onto the point itself. The artillery of the paratroops is the airforce, and it was over this that Tull and I really put our heads together, as it was obvious we were in for one of the biggest massacres of villagers seen for some time unless we could stop some of the projected bombing. Both of us were sure we were going to get the objective, if not without opposition then at any rate with the minimum of it, and that from the Point only. We saw no object in rubbing out two or three villages unnecessarily. I spoke to Maj.-Gen. Down on the subject, who told me, to quote his own words, that "he wouldn't in the least bit mind killing 500 villagers to save one Gurkha's life." With this view I strongly disagree, the villagers after all being members of the Empire and therefore under our protection. But I disagreed even more because that point of view was not even militarily sound. In the long run certainly and in the short run too, probably, you will lose more soldiers' lives by that method. However, I didn't think it worthwhile arguing the point.

Now the air was being controlled by Edward Tull and his team - that was what they were there for. As, however, it was the first time that they had tried this out, the army 'weren't taking any risks' (i.e. of Tull failing to get touch with the air) and so devised a most incredibly complicated bombing programme:

> Strategic bombing. This consisted of 96 Liberators which were going down on Elephant Point and 48 Mitchells which were going down on the end of Ywathitkon. This bombing was going down no matter what happened, and was NOT to be controlled from the ground or even to have communication with the ground.

> Tactical bombing and strafing. Consisted of Mitchells and Thunderbolts and was going in on a timed programme on Tawkalaik and Thaunggon UNLESS CANCELLED FROM THE GROUND.

The 'cab rank,' so called because you could call it up if required. It consisted of Mustangs and Mosquitos which cruised about overhead, ready to engage any targets indicated by Tull from the ground, but were not to engage any targets on their own.

Thus we had one type of support which was going down whatever happened; one which was going down unless cancelled; and one which would not go down unless ordered. The Liberators going down on Elephant Point were welcome to it: it consisted only of mangrove, and Japanese bunkers and they were welcome to put 10,000 tons on that if they wanted. The 48 Mitchells going to Ywathitkon unfortunately could not be stopped. The tactical airforce was due to wipe out Tawkalaik, Thaunggon and the near half of Ywathitkon unless prevented. Clearly, therefore, if things proceeded according to plan and nothing done about it, there was going to be a most frightful massacre of villagers. We reckoned the harvest would probably be 250 killed: a grisly prospect, so Tull and I arranged that:

1. I should go full bat for Tawkai (as explained above, when it came to it Tawkai came to me instead) in order to get the very earliest possible information about the Japs.

2. I should send a villager full steam to Elephant Point to warn all villagers to run into the paddy fields and stay there all day until we arrived.

3. Tull would make sure of getting communication with the air and preventing any unnecessary bombing and strafing.

It was fortunate that our plans, which admittedly were made by ourselves, far from being at variance with our official duties, were essential to them. It was my job to get the information, Tull's to get communication with the air, and we were not warning the enemy, as they could not possibly fail to see the colossal armada which was due to come in in broad daylight. Tull and I hoped that with reasonable luck we should save any loss of life among the villagers, and save all the villages except the far end of Ywathitkon.

The only thing which need be added, on the question of plans, is that in the afternoon we were due to take in our sappers. They were not coming in on the original wave, but were coming in on the same DZ that afternoon.

And now, what actually happened? We got some sleep on the night of the 30th, but were woken at 1 am on May 1st and marched to the aerodrome, about a mile distant. We had all of course been told off to aircraft earlier in the day, and our kit and fitted parachutes had already been dumped there. We were going down with 'valises,' which are excellent things. They are canvas bags which are strapped to your right leg, and have 40 feet of stout cord, one end of which is attached to the bag and the other end to your parachute harness. You can get quite a fair amount of stuff into it. You go out, then when you are airborne and have adjusted all twists etc. you pull the quick release, the valise comes loose from your leg and you lower it down to the full extent of the rope. It then dangles below you as you go down. This not only means that it is not on your leg when you land, which would be very awkward, but tends to give you an easier landing as, just before you get down, 60 lbs weight is taken off the parachute.

The pathfinder aircraft took off about 2 am. The dropping aircraft were all USAAF and ours was piloted by the colonel in charge of the whole force, Col. McCulloch I think his name was - a most competent and helpful bloke who put us bung on the bull. I should have liked to have thanked him, but, as expected, had to leave him in rather a hurry. I was going No. 5 in our aircraft (and all 21 were going in one stick - there was to be no second run over the target) so was sitting third seat up on the port (door) side. We had two despatchers, one of whom was American and one RAF. I occupied myself in my usual manner on these occasions, viz, singing hymns at the top of my voice. My next door neighbours bore it with great fortitude, though it is open to doubt if I shall get away with it if I ever have to bale out from jets, and there isn't the roar of the fans to act as a counterblast to my efforts.

We hugged the coast all the way down until we were clear of the last of the Yomas, and then cut across the Delta. It probably wasn't a very difficult operation from the aircraft's point of view, but that doesn't alter the fact that the job could not have been done better. We turned for the target, were given just right time to put on parachutes and hook up, got just the right amount of warning and went down on the bull on the dot of time. There was no circling, no sign of the aircraft.

There was one rather amusing incident as we went out. The order was to be: two packages first, one with Tull's wireless set in it, then the war correspondent, then Tull, then the rest of us. Before you go you get a red light for warning then a few seconds later a green for go. In a few seconds an aircraft going at 120 mph can go quite a long way, at least so it will seem to you on the ground when you are doing it on foot! Well, the red went, and as it went the despatcher pushed out the packages. I was by no means disinterested as the other package contained my pack. Being a Bergen rucksack it wouldn't go in my valise. I caught up with it that evening. I didn't want it before, as I had my equipment and necessities for the day either on me or in my valise. Tull turned on him and shouted "You are a bloody fool: that will be a devil of a way..." "Go!!!" shouted the despatcher, as the green came on, and exit Tull, thereby terminating the argument quicker than I've ever seen one terminated before.

It was, of course, broad daylight when we went out, and we were just the right height. I got a good take-off, but for some reason got about eight spins. Nobody, I believe, really knows why people get spins, and I don't believe it has anything to do with your take-off. They are not in the least serious, as all you do is unwind them, though until you have done so you may go down rather quicker than normally. I don't think I was in the air more than half a minute, and hardly felt myself touch the ground. We were on paddy which had been rendered beautifully soft by early rain, and in addition I had my blanket inside the seat of my trousers, as usual. I recommend this to anyone thinking of taking up parachuting as a hobby. You've got to take your blanket somewhere; why not take it where it is protecting you and neither is it taking up space in your equipment.

We all landed well, the villagers all came up in a great mass, all wildly excited: I soon got into touch with Force 136, who confirmed that there were no Japs about: so I sent off a villager to tell all villagers to get out of their villages and stay out all day. Had he done what I told him to, I think we might have got away with it altogether. But he must have funked it at the last moment, for Ywathitkon was not warned, and as a result we had 24 killed there, but that was all, and was only one tenth of what we had expected. But this is anticipating.

I found Tull, who had his flares and had also found his set! and all we then had to do was wait for the armada. This arrived bung on time, Tull lit the flares and they came dead at us. In some ways it was the most thrilling sight of the war. There were 42 aircraft, in absolutely perfect formation, all in arrowheads of three aircraft, with about half a mile between arrowheads - all in a plumb straight line, and all at the same height. And out they came, right over our heads, each arrowhead disgorging its human contents at exactly the same spot. It looked, of course, as if the second wave was going to cut the first lot of parachutists to ribbons, and so on, but by the time the second wave was dropping the first lot were down 150 feet. Layer after layer came down, one on top of the other, and the spectacle was made even more picturesque by reason of the different coloured parachutes, indicating which particular weapon or store they were carrying. I cheered heartily. The villagers got on with the more serious business of swiping all the parachutes: we were both in our respective elements.

Having mushed up, we formed up in Tawkai and prepared to move off. I had asked leave to go with the advanced scout section, being the only Burmese speaker, and this was granted. I knew the chances of meeting any Japs were nil, and wanted to be able to warn any villagers we saw. About six villagers attached themselves to me, so we were a composite section of one major, one naik (corporal), seven Gurkhas, two Indian shopkeepers and four Burmese peasants. After that came Brighton beach on August bank holiday. It could hardly be expected to look like anything else. Troops had to spread out into open formation, and as there was absolutely no cover, it being paddy, you could see them all. We made good progress, and had got through Tawkalaik well ahead of time when we were halted, and after half an hours halt were called back! The reason for this, however, should have been obvious to me, but was, none the less, a defect in the plan. The tactical bombing on Tawkalaik (which I was glad to see was deserted) was not due for some time yet, and if Tull failed to get communication, would possibly come down with us there. So we were ordered to wait until it was certain that it had been cancelled. Actually, I think that they should have gone on. Every section had a bright orange umbrella, and when our aircraft came over these were put up to indicate the position of our forward troops. Anyway, the orders were to wait.

Tull in due course got communication - he never failed once throughout the day - the bombing was stopped, one village was saved, and on we went.

We were about half way between Tawkalaik and Thaunggon, when over came the Liberators, 96 of them in all, bombing Elephant Point singly. They took about an hour in all, and were carrying some pretty big stuff, judging by the noise and columns of water which came up. In the middle of the bombing, however, there was a first class tragedy. One of the Liberators, owing to a technical fault we were afterwards told, loosed its bombs three miles short and six 1000 lb bombs fell straight across a company in the open some 300 yards from where I was standing: 17 killed and 25 wounded, including three British officers badly wounded. This, of course, involved further delay, and as soon after that the Mitchells were due to go in on Ywathitkon, we waited for them too. It was pathetic to see all those houses go up, but they were part of the strategic bombers and we could not stop them. After that there was yet one more delay as the Thunderbolts were due to go in on Thaunggon, which was just ahead of us. Tull called them up alright, but they were evidently only prepared to compromise, as though they did not drop bombs they gave the village a few 'squirts' (the correct technical term, I believe), and I was glad to note when we went through it that the villagers had fled to the paddy fields.

We did move on then, and had got through Thaunggon when we met the unfortunate villagers coming back from Ywathitkon. It was heartbreaking to see them. Luckily there were very few wounded, and those there were we attended to. After they had calmed down a bit I gave them a talk saying how sorry I was about it all, how we had tried

to warn them, how war caused suffering to all, but that the war for
Burma was practically over as the Japanese were retreating and would
never be able to come back. I then went on to say that when the
government came back they would then attend to them properly, but in
the meantime I wanted to do what I could to help them, on behalf of
the government, and gave them 7000 rupees (Not, repeat Not, my
own!) in Burmese money, to help rebuild their villages. You've no idea
how this cheered things up. I didn't exactly get a hand, but they were
obviously vastly relieved, and we parted on terms of mutual cordial
esteem.

It was now about 1 pm, and the CO sent me back to help with the
afternoon drop - ref coolies etc., and also to bring up the wounded. So I
did not see the actual capture of the Point, but to complete the picture I
will give a secondhand account of what happened.

It was reported that there were Japs in a boat in a small inlet just
north of Ywathitkon. It was afterwards established that this was a party
of some 25 Japanese fleeing from Rangoon to Moulmein by boat, who
had put in to Ywathitkon for the day and who would presumably have
moved off that night. They were not the garrison of Elephant Point.
There were reports that some of them got into Ywathitkon and started
sniping, but this was not confirmed. But 25 did get into one bunker
(stupid fools) north of Ywathitkon. Tull managed to get one of his 'cab
rank' cannon-firing Mosquitos onto it. After seeing one of these attack
another bunker which was suspected of having Japs in it, I'm glad I
wasn't in the bunker. He went in in a shallow dive, flying as slowly as
possible, and opened fire at about 800 yards. He went on firing until he
was only 200 yards away, by which time a fair amount of the cannon
shells were going through the slit. You can't do much about that if
you're inside. The target being indicated by smoke bombs fired from 3"
mortars, and that made a pretty fair mess of things. It was finished off
by the Gurkhas with a flame-thrower in a small but gallant action
which resulted in four of our men being killed, including one officer.
Elephant Point fell during the course of the afternoon.

And now, before I go back to fetch the wounded, I'm going to say
what I think about the attack. As we got Elephant Point, and as we
killed the 25 Japs who were there, one is apt to overlook the fact that it
could have been a far more protracted and bitter business than it was.
The whole area was studded with very powerful bunkers, well
constructed with teak posts and struts, and enough earth to resist
anything but a direct hit from a bomb, or a flame-thrower, or very
accurate cannon fire. There were some bunkers at and around all the
villages we passed through, and a really large concentration of bunkers
(about 25) in the immediate area of Elephant Point itself. They weren't
in an unduly extended area - most of them were in a circle of 500 yards

diameter, yet the 96 Liberators had only knocked-out three!

Experience has shown that you cannot knock-out bunkers by pattern bombing. The way to knock-out bunkers is to take one bunker at a time, indicate it by smoke - 3" mortar smoke - and then send Mustang or Thunderbolt dive bombers on it. Given good indication one Mustang out of three should get a direct hit, and then you move on to the next bunker. But you must be prepared to take a bunker position slowly or have a fearful loss of life. Flame-throwers will be all right in the jungle, but on an open stretch like Elephant Point would be too expensive. Luckily such Japs as were there committed the supreme fully of all getting in one bunker. If even that lot had divided up to say three a bunker, things might have been very tiresome for a bit. Bravery is no use if tactics are wrong. Tull's control of the air throughout was first class, and the team he had with him knew their job backwards.

I took some time to get back, as it was some distance, and I found, at Tawkai, the QM with a large number of stores and - luckily simply thousands of locals. I can't imagine where so many had come from, but I presume the double lure of excitement and parachute silk, particularly the latter, had done the trick. Anyway, they were very welcome, as there were loads of stores to be got forward, and it took some time arranging for the necessary carts and carriers. However, it was done at last, and we started to move forward to a hamlet just short of Thaunggon. There were a few more injured by this time, as the hot weather wind had got up by the time the afternoon flight came in, and I think four broke their arms as a result of going sideways into houses.

We got the stuff dumped and the coolies paid off by about 5 pm, and then had to get forward to Elephant Point with the wounded, as the Doc was already there plus some of the wounded. So I put the wounded on bullock carts, and off we went. By the time we had reached the near end of Ywathitkon it was pitch dark, and there we met the Doc, plus stretcher bearers, plus the other wounded. He said he had been told there were snipers in the village, the far half of which was still smouldering, anyway, and that we were to go round by the right, and that the man in front knew the way: how often have I heard that one before! Well, the wounded needed attention, the Doc needed to get to Elephant Point to give it to them, and so we started to go round to the right, which was mangrove. We struggled on, in the pitch dark, shoving and sweating, but mangrove is not the ideal surface for bullock carts, and we made very slow progress. After a time it came on to rain and there was some lightning. This wasn't an unmixed curse, as we could see the Elephant Point signalling derrick about 600 yards away. We made even slower progress in and after the rain, and after a bit the Doc and I arranged I'd go forward with two carts and the stretcher bearers and when I'd got them to the Point I'd come back with some help. we struggled up to some 40 yards from the Point, when we were greeted with volleys of LMG fire and grenades. Presumably the troops had not been warned we were coming, and may well have been a bit jumpy after the heavy losses they'd had from bombing. None the less, it was extremely unpleasant, particularly as they had, apparently, an unlimited supply of Verey lights which they fired off almost continuously, and which showed as up a clear as crystal. Needless to say, we hollered out who we were, but even so it took a very unpleasant ten minutes to stop them, during which I heard we had one killed and four wounded: it was most unfortunate. The thing that saved us was the mud. Needless to say we were all lying well down in it, and the grenades, of which there were ample thrown, all sank well into the mud before exploding. We stopped them at last, got that lot of wounded in, returned and brought in the rest, and then I just lay down as I was, wrapped myself up, and slept.

Half way through the night it not only came on to rain hard, but we had one of the heaviest thunderstorms I've ever been in. We could hardly have been more exposed than we were, and I'm surprised nobody was struck. I suppose the high steel derrick protected us. Anyway, I wasn't worrying much by then. I was very tired, still very angry, and pulled the blanket over my head and slept deeply until the morning.

Our job was done, and all that remained was to straighten things out. Early the following morning the invasion armada sailed up the river, but its job was not to take Rangoon but to land on each bank of the river some ten miles up from the mouth. This they hadn't much difficulty in doing, on our bank at any rate, as there were no Japs there. There wasn't many on the other side either, and both landings were effected all right. Most unfortunately one LCT struck a mine some three miles up the river and sank with heavy loss of life. We could clearly see half of it sticking up out of the water. Edward Tull and I started the day by hoisting the Union Jack from the Elephant Point derrick, and most of the rest of the day I was busied with arranging for labour. Also we sent the wounded off by boat. That evening I had a very pleasant dinner with the headman of Thaunggon: it was a great improvement on our rations.

The day after was much the same, and the day after that, for some reason I could not quite fathom, we were to march up the west bank of the river, and this we did, in a long straggling line through a good deal of mangrove. I managed to bag a russell's viper on the way up, after it had made a valiant attempt to bite one of the villagers who was with us. We got boats to cross the Pilakat Chaung, slogged on a few more miles - with the aid of some rain - got more boats to cross the Bassein Creek, and caught up with the troops who were on the west bank and who were becoming somewhat sceptical about the feasibility of carrying out their allotted task, which was to build a Spitfire strip! as there was 18 inches of liquid mud and the prospect of the whole monsoon to come. There were also audacious spirits - a good many, in fact, who suggested that it might be easier just to go up and take Rangoon, particularly as it was known the Japs had gone. This highly dashing line of action eventually became so popular that the Spitfire strip idea was abandoned and the decision taken to go up to Rangoon then and there. I suggested to the CO that I had done my job and might as well go to Rangoon, and when he agreed we parted with expressions of mutual esteem. So I jumped the last LCT and at 7 pm we drew alongside Brooking Street wharf, and I slept the night on board. The day after I walked up to Government House and reported to Force 136. There was nothing to do so I spent two days walking round Rangoon surveying the damage, and on 7th May flew back to Calcutta. When I reached Colombo, some few days later, I read the account of the state of Rangoon which had been sent to the Ceylon Times officially by the army and was by our "Military Correspondent." While it did not contain any single lie of quite the Himalayan grandeur of the one about the Sittang crossing, it was clear as daylight it had been written by a man who knew just what sort of lies the public wanted to hear and was going to give it to them. As an example of cheap sensation-mongering it could hardly be surpassed, and coming from an authoritative and official source was a disgrace to the department which produced it. I wrote through my HQ to SEAC to tell them so, but don't suppose the letter got very far. Truly, in war the first casualty is truth.

Operation Dracula was over, and Rangoon was ours once more. As I've said before, it should never have been put on at all, in my opinion, but once prepared to reconcile oneself to being on an unnecessary operation, it had its moments of interest and excitement, and certainly taught me a lot, and I saw a few more places I'd never have seen otherwise. I'm glad I went on it, but wish what we did had been rather more essential, and not quite so wasteful in lives and materials.

The Interval

As soon as I arrived back in Calcutta I asked to be sent home on compassionate grounds (I had mooted this some time previously) then to have the rest of my 61 days' leave in Simla with my wife and daughter, and then to be transferred to the Siam section of 136. Some time before that I had seen the cloud about the size of a man's hand on the horizon, and that cloud was CAS(B). Whatever happened I was determined not to get into that show, but knew I'd have to be able to produce a pretty good reason why I should not be hoofed into CAS(B) whether I liked it or not. Luckily I was armour-plated, as I could say with perfect truth I was a Siamese speaker. I had recently, in my spare time, been relearning my Siamese, and found that I had not forgotten much since I left Siam in 1934. As Siamese speakers were few and far between, I was accepted by the management, and promptly left for Colombo. There I stayed until on 29th May 1945 I flew from Ratmalana aerodrome for England in a York. In the same aircraft was Dick Musgrave (late BBTCL) who was relinquishing command of our school at Horana. He had done a first class job of work there, and was a very fine officer.

The flight home was most interesting. We took off at 7 am from Ratmalana, and touched down, without a stop, at Karachi at about 3 pm. We had an early tea there, and went to bed, as we were to be up at 2 am to take off again. It was boiling hot, but I was thankful to see a huge thundercloud rolling up on us, and was reflecting how pleasant it would be when the storm broke.

We left the flaps of our tent open to remain a bit cooler, but were just waiting for the storm. It came about half an hour later, but was sand! We got very little sleep! We took off at 2 am, and had breakfast at Shaibah, which must be the last place ever created. Blisteringly hot, in the middle of a flat desert, nothing anywhere except sand - quite useless for training in jungle warfare!

We took off just before 11 am, one of the engines having given trouble, and it was lucky we did get off then, as, owing to the heat, aircraft are not allowed to take off after 11 am for fear of boiling, and we should have had to wait until the following morning. That was the most interesting part of the journey. To start off, and for a long time we travelled over miles and miles of near-desert, very heavily cut by nullahs - for there is so little vegetation that when rain does fall, which happens from time to time, there is nothing to hold it and it tears a way through everything. There was some scrub, but the most interesting part was later on. The whole land looked to be in layers. The hills had, of course, been heavily weathered, and you could see these layers, one on top of another, and all of varied colours - really very beautiful. We then went over the Dead Sea, and if ever I've seen a place which looked like the mouth of hell, it was the east side of that sea. The rocks were almost black, looked as sharp as razors, utterly devoid of vegetation, and looked, and I have no shadow of doubt were - boiling hot. Down they went, cliff above cliff, down and down, to the sea at the bottom, ringed by sand and more sand. One could well imagine the pitiless heat down there. I hope I never bale out there! We went over southern Palestine, which looked desolate enough, in all conscience though not quite as bad as the land we had been over, over the Suez Canal, stretching away as far as the eye could see in both directions. Soon after that - what a change - green fields, houses - the Valley of the Nile, with its irrigation canals laid out as neatly as a geometrical drawing. One couldn't see a better example of the value of water than by flying over that fearful desert and then suddenly coming back onto that prosperous and fertile valley. We saw the Pyramids in the distance, and shortly afterwards landed at Cairo West, some 15 miles west of the city. We spent another short night there: took off at 2 am, breakfasted at Malta, and by 4 pm were in England, having landed near Swindon. It took me 60 hours overall time from Colombo to my home near Godalming. Not bad going.

I was at home for just three weeks. During that time, apart from personal matters, I went to report to Force 136 HQ. Under their direction I visited various schools and training establishments, and also the "Museum." What I saw there must, I am afraid, still remain secret, but suffice it to say that I saw some of the most diabolically clever machines and devices it has ever been my lot to clap eyes on, and wish I could have been there longer. When HM the King visited the Museum, he was to remain for 45 minutes but did, in fact, remain two-and-a-half hours! I'm glad those tricks were on our side and not the enemy's!

6
Siam

I returned to Karachi in what, in my opinion, is the steadiest aircraft I've ever travelled in - a short Sunderland Flying Boat of BOAC. I've never been in any aircraft which gave such a feeling of rock-like firmness. It never seemed to move in the air at all. Being a flying boat we came back, of course, by a different route: Poole-Marseilles-Catania-Cairo-Habbaniya-Bahrein- Karachi.

After two days in Karachi I flew to Delhi, spent a night there and then went up to Simla for the rest of my 61 days' leave. I had still five days to run when I was recalled to Ceylon for urgent duty. So I took the train to Ceylon, and reported in due course to Horana.

First of all I was going to join the Siam section of Force 136, then that fell through; then I was going to bale out over Malaya to help POW's. Then the atomic bomb fell, and soon after that the war fizzled out and my prospect of any job with Force 136 with it. They told me they had no job for me, but that 207 British Military Mission had asked for me, being a Siamese speaker and I was to report to them. So with great regret I left Force 136. That type of work, which is exciting, out of the usual run, and of a nature which gives almost endless scope for imagination and initiative, is just the sort of work which appeals to me, and I only wish I'd had more of it. They were grand people to work for, and amongst other things had the advantage of not being a regular army unit for questions of pay etc. This made it possible to settle such questions rapidly and personally, rather than laboriously through the correct channels. I need hardly say I have made many life-long friends in this Unit - as I did in others.

Siam - 207 British Military Mission

The war was over - both wars were over. So any job one took on from now on could only be at most a job of rounding up Jap deserters turned bandits, but would far more probably be one of garrison or staff duties. In the circumstances, I don't think I could have had a better job, for, danger alone barred, my job with 207 BMM was the most varied and interesting job I've ever done in my life.

I left Horana, went up to Kandy, where I reported to - and took my leave of - Force 136 HQ, and then reported, at ALFSEA HQ, to my new Brigadier, A. Wilson Brand, and met his G1, Lt.-Col. Kenny, who soon handed over to Lt-Col. Carter, Major W. Brooks, MC and bar, who was to be our G2(I) and Lt.-Col. P.B. Kirrage, OBE (BBTCL up-country Siam) who was our A&Q. I shall introduce the other members of the Mission as and when occasion arises. We spent a few days in Kandy collecting stores etc. and also finding out what our job was to be when we arrived in Siam.

We moved off a few days later, having been joined by a bluff, hearty Australian by name Major L. Coffey, who before the war had been prospecting for tin in southern Siam. We went by train and ferry to Madras, stayed there one or two nights and then flew in another of those rock-like Sunderlands to Rangoon, where we landed at Syriam. We spent two nights in a rest camp at Mingaladon, waiting for the Armistice to be officially signed in Tokyo, as until that were signed we were not able to move.

And while we're waiting to go I might as well say a few words about the prospects. Our GOC was Maj.-Gen. Evans, CB, CBE, DSO, and his troops were 7th Ind Div. The task of the Div was primarily to take over and disarm the Japanese in Siam and repatriate Allied POWs, but there were of course a whole lot more jobs as well. There were members of the Indian National Army (INA) in Siam; there was Siam itself - still technically an enemy; there was the question of British internees; British property and loss of same, and a whole host of other questions. Needless to say, this entailed a very large HQ, for in addition to the Div HQ, there were all sorts and kinds of specialist officers, and on top of that Bangkok became a sub-area HQ with a complete sub-area staff. The prime job of the Mission was liaison between the British HQ and the Siamese Army and Government. There were other jobs on the directive, but they were all to the same end. The last of our jobs, however, is worth noting: it was "The training and re-equipping of the Siamese Army." I was asked what I thought about this, as were other Siam men, and we said in no uncertain terms that if that were to be our job we were to be there for 10,000 years if it were to be done well. "Oh No!" we were told, "This is the New Siam!" We all said that we were content to wait and see. It took the management about a week to find out that the Siamese Army would never be an army by our standards, and the attempt to retrain and re-equip them was very soon relegated to the limbo of forgotten things. There was also one job which was not, unless my memory is at fault, on the original directive but which we did do, and that was the disarming of the Japanese Army. I shall have masses more to say about these subjects in due course, but I would like the reader to realise what we were expecting to do when we first went in.

We started the fly-in from Hmawbi airfield on September 3rd. To get there we had to motor past the scene of the Taukkyan roadblock, and I remembered just how different it had looked the last time I had seen it.

We were not able to fly in the whole Div at once, so the first day Advanced Div HQ, the Mission, and about one battalion went in. The weather was bumpy and bad in Burma, in fact one or two aircraft got into difficulties, but there were no crashes on that first day although regrettably there were several later on. The weather over those hills in September can be very bad. However, the weather over Siam was fine, and we made a perfect landing on the Don Muang aerodrome, a fine 1500 yard runway some 14 miles north of Bangkok.

We had been warned before going in that though it was thought the Japanese would honour the terms of the surrender, their attitude was not known for certain, and as they could have massacred the whole lot of us without difficulty when we first landed, we were given strict instructions that an absolutely correct attitude to the Japanese was to be observed, and also that there was to be no commandeering of transport. I have set this out at some length as it helps to add further lustre to the shining examples set by two people, one known to be an army officer, the other unknown but probably an RAF man. I'll take the second first.

The Japs had perfectly correctly detailed a full colonel to report as liaison officer to Maj.-Gen. Evans when he landed. He was waiting, correctly dressed and with his sword, in one of the hangars. There he was found by X, who without warning went up to him and kicked him in the stomach, pulled off his shoulder titles, took his sword, ONE boot, and was never caught. I imagine he was RAF to have made such a clean getaway.

The other was known and caught. He was the Army Public Relations Officer. He went into Bangkok and found his was to Japanese GHQ. There he said he wanted a car, and had all available cars paraded for his inspection. Not being satisfied with any of them he called for the Japanese GOC-in-C's personal car. This, apparently, was satisfactory, so he drove off in it.

It just goes to show how much sense of responsibility some people have got. Luckily, however, the Japanese did not decide to massacre the whole lot of us.

The General established his HQ at the aerodrome, where there are some excellent buildings, and we, with some troops, went into Bangkok. We were driven in on Jap lorries driven by Jap drivers, and got a tremendous ovation from the proletariat. We returned their salutations with interest and it was while we were doing this that the driver took a hump-backed bridge at 35/40 mph. Everything left the floor by three feet, which must have given the driver considerable pleasure. We called him a long string of names which needn't be detailed here, but I should have thought him a spineless maggot if he hadn't done it.

Meanwhile, a considerable number of our POWs had been billeted near the aerodrome and were sent back to India in the empty aircraft. They, and others I saw subsequently, were in the finest physical condition of any man I've ever seen, the reason being, of course, that the weakest had died, poor fellows, and only the strong remained.

We arrived at the Ratanakosin hotel, a large modern hotel near the Royal palace which had been entirely taken over for the British troops. The first thing that happened was that we were entertained to a colossal official 'thiophene.' Everybody was of course delighted to see everybody else and nothing was too much trouble.

After lunch the Brigadier, Peter Kirrage and myself, plus a Siamese LO of the name of Col. Kamrawn, who was a very decent bloke - ex-West Point - went round to meet the Siamese C-in-C; a courtesy visit. And the moment I saw that old boy I knew my bet was won. A perfect old darling, guaranteed to smile for 24 hours on end should occasion demand it, a smash hit at giving the prizes away at speech day at the kindergarten, utterly useless at anything pertaining to the military art, great or small; incapable of commanding a section or an army corps or any intermediate formation, but a dear old boy. We were given copious draughts of soda water while the C-in-C tried to get the smile to meet at the back of his neck, and then we departed. As we went out, Peter and I decided that the old order had definitely not passed away. We knew what we were dealing with and both contemplated with smug satisfaction the prospect of the management finding it out in due course - which they did.

We settled in the Ratanakosin, which was up to date and comfortable, and lived off the fat of the land. After two days I was sent out as LO between the Mission and the GOC, sleeping at Mingaladon every night and spending most of the day on various jobs in Bangkok. Meanwhile, more stores and personnel were being flown in and more ex-POWs flown out. One of my first jobs for the General was to make out a map of where the Jap forces were in Bangkok. After three more days we moved into Bangkok, where GHQ was established at the Anurat palace, just opposite the Dusit racecourse. This was a most magnificent building, and Bangkok had of course the great advantage over say Rangoon of not having been looted. Needless to say the Siamese, knowing on which side their bread was buttered, did us proud. I remained as LO and stayed in the Anurat palace by night, spending my days with the Mission or dashing around town on a variety of errands. The GOC had full dress conferences morning and evening which were attended by representatives of all formations and units in Bangkok, so everyone knew what was going on everywhere else if he kept his eyes and ears open.

This was quite an interesting period, but it was not what I personally had gone to Siam for. After a few days the great loathing which this war has given me for all towns and HQs was beginning to assert itself and I was not sorry when I was told that on 13th September I was to report to 37 Div (Siamese) in Korat as LO. There were six divisions (for lack of a better word) of Siamese troops (also for lack of a better word), and 37 was an independent division responsible for the whole of Paksam, which means "Province No. 3" and is the whole eastern plateau. As can be seen from a glance at a map of Siam, there is a range of hills running north and south to the north-east of Bangkok. They are not high but are pretty bad going, being covered in thick jungle in many places, and they form an effective barrier.[1]

So Paksam, the Eastern province, is a much more isolated province than other provinces of Siam. Once on the plateau it is dead flat with paddy and jungle ad infinitum. The main town, or capital, of this huge province is Korat, near its western boundary. Here was the seat of government and also the Army HQ. We went up by train, which took 12 hours. I was given an interpreter/LO, a flight-lieutenant in the Siamese air force, and he did actually get as far as Ubon. He was quite a decent fellow but a typical Bangkok glamour boy and quite useless as far as I was concerned. I sent him back after a week, which was a great joy to him and an unbounded relief to me.

Except that I was to be LO with 37 Div I don't think I had any explicit orders, apart from that I was to ensure that "at all times there were sufficient Siamese troops to ensure my personal safety!" Had I paid any attention to this, which of course I did not, I should have found any form of movement absolutely out of the question. There was not enough transport to cart around masses of troops with me, and no Siamese troops would have kept up for 50 yards with me walking. So, when I went to Korat I was not exactly sure of what I was going to do. The management still thought we were going to retrain and re-equip the Siamese Army, that mighty stabilising force in South-East Asia, and so for the time being I was to get into touch with the Siamese Army, find out where their streamlined armoured divisions were, where were their permanent stations, training grounds of their paratroop brigades etc. I was under no delusions, and as it will be 12 hours before we reach Korat perhaps it would be as well to explain to my readers a little

---

1   It may be of interest that the Japanese had they failed to hold our advance into Siam from the west were not going to attempt to fight in Siam's central plain, but were going to pull back and hold the line of the Korat hills. With this end in view, they had, with our POW labour, built a formidable line of defences in the hills. They also freely admitted that had war come to Siam they were going to murder all our officer POW's to prevent them helping Siamese patriot forces. They knew these existed, but were satisfied they would be useless unless led by BO's.

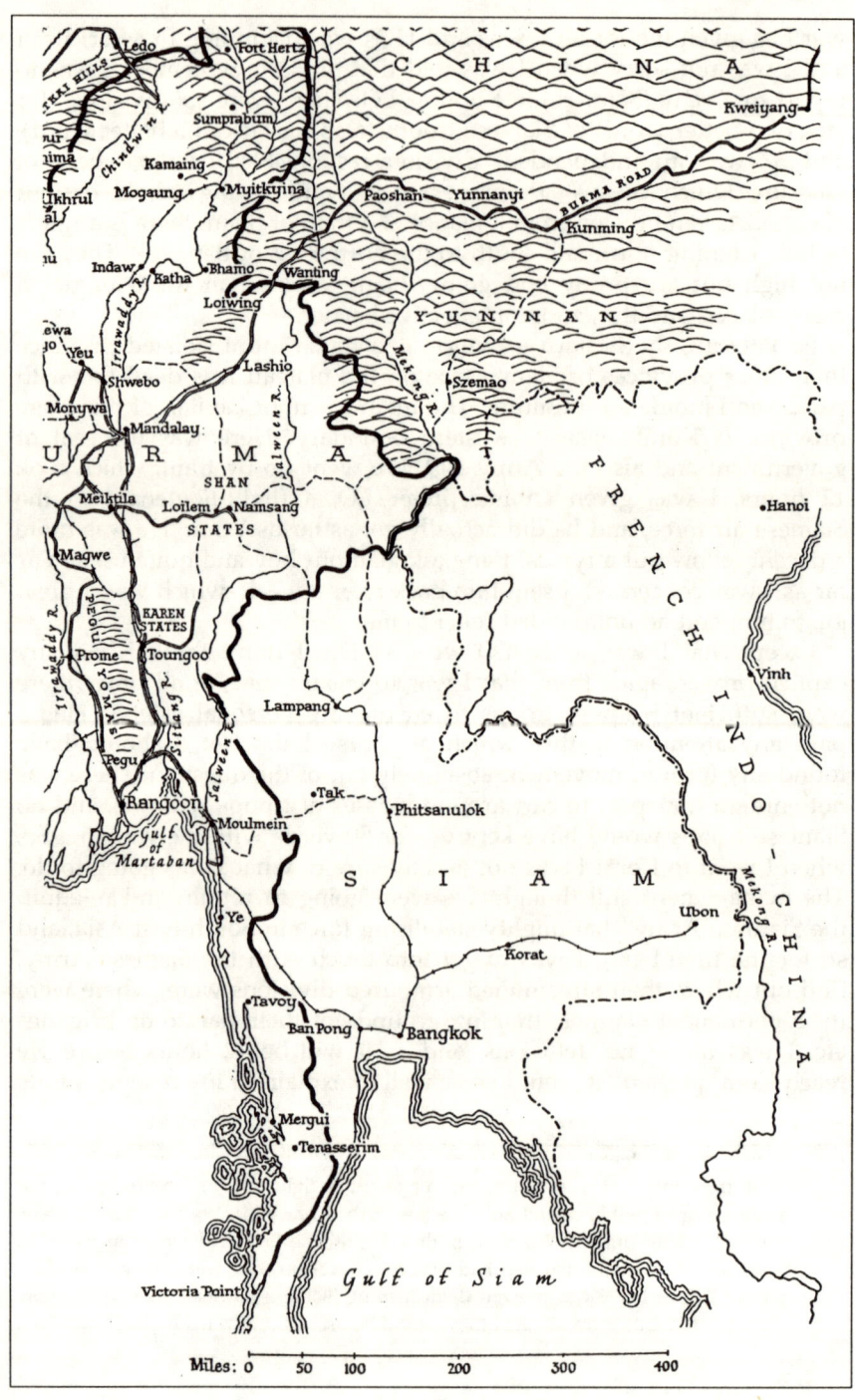

about Siam and the Siamese Army.

Siam, like Burma, is a large country for the size of its population and is almost entirely agricultural. Consequently, as would be expected, the people are simple, kindly, easy going and perfectly content with little. They have no ambitions other than to be left in peace in their villages, to cultivate the fields and to be given some comforts - not many - and reasonable freedom from dacoity and oppression. They don't really ask much, and in this they are encouraged by the Buddhist religion, which teaches the uselessness of great riches, and the weather which, being hot and sultry, discourages hard work and industry. Their whole outlook is intensely parochial. They are very much interested in what goes on in their own villages and, in their villages, capable of managing their affairs well. For that reason they are most concerned in whether the Nai Amphurs (head of the village tract) and the Ka Luangs (provincial governor) are people who try to understand and help them or whether they make life burdensome by taking large bribes. By and large the Nai Amphurs and Ka Luangs are thoroughly decent fellows. They may take their bit - this has become so recognised, up to a point, as not to be the least bit resented - but they are in touch with the land, they do know that the villagers are their people, and that the latter's welfare is their welfare, and I believe they do their best. They may not always be very up to date, and of course everything in Siam takes time, everyone accepts that as so obvious as to be almost desirable, as it preserves the even tenor of life, avoiding rush and bother, but the spirit is there, and that is what really matters. Their wants being so little, and being able to grow all their own food, Siam can run almost entirely on its provincial administration, for it is the provincial administration alone which actively concerns the peasant, who is 95% of the whole population. Consequently, it is not surprising that the peasants have absolutely no interest whatsoever in what goes on in Bangkok or parliament, or any nonsense about democracy or such claptrap as that.

And therein lies Siam's danger, for therein lies a potential danger to the great mass of the simple Siamese peasantry. Until 1932 Siam was an absolute monarchy and the peasantry well-governed through the hierarchy, which began at the village headman and ended up at the king. In 1932 there was the first of what turned out to be a series of petty revolutions, culminating in the abdication of the then king, Prajadipok, and the setting up of what on the face of it was a democratically elected assembly, but which in fact was no such thing. In the first place the average villager had not - and still has not - the foggiest idea of what he is doing when he casts his vote, and any politician can hoodwink the peasantry without the slightest difficulty. As is usually the case in most countries politics tends to attract a poor type of person, largely out for his own ends and lacking - particularly in an eastern country - the sense of real civic responsibility without which democracy becomes a tragic farce. But far worse than this, ever since the first revolution has been the consistent and utterly baneful influence of the army, always exerted behind the scenes. Although it is quite useless as a fighting force, the army is strong enough to terrorise the local inhabitants, or, if it comes to that, Bangkok itself. Its power is not wielded openly. A politician says something which the army does not like, and a few days later he is arrested for leaving his car outside the cinema parked too far from the kerb, and it may be 12 months before his case is heard, during the whole of which time he is in detention. Free speech and free criticism become meaningless while this sort of thing is going on, and will continue to do so as long as the political power of the army remains unbroken. Consequently, in Bangkok one sees the loathsome spectacle of endless jockeying for position. There is the police party, the air force party, the army party and a whole lot more, and government is carried on as a result of a series of dishonest checks and compromises arrived at as the result of the parleyings, jockeyings and backstairs politics of the various groups - the army group always being the dominating factor. Because the mass of the common people care nothing for Bangkok or what goes on there, what they say and think means nothing there. Partly through ignorance and partly through concentration on their local affairs, they have for the time being surrendered their freedom - potentially at any rate - to the politicians, official and unofficial, in Bangkok.

What is the result of this? Just what you would expect. Each group is out for its own good, the army for a large grant every year from the budget, and so on, and that at present is where the country's money is going. It is not entirely selfishness. It is as well to remember that the educated Siamese still look back to the golden age of the Siamese kings when, around about 1300 AD the Siamese Empire stretched from Pegu to the Mekong River, and from the southern borders of China to what is now Singapore. They are intensely proud of their past and jealously proud that, with the exception of Japan, they have been for years past the only independent country in the Far East. Furthermore, and this is perhaps an even more important point, their point of view is very narrow. Few have been outside the country, and hardly any are aware of how insignificant a power in the world is Siam today; and their powers of self-deception are almost unlimited. In nothing is this more apparent than in the Siamese attitude to the recent war (1939-45). As is generally known, Siam resisted (?) the Japanese for six hours, and then, under Japanese pressure and aided by the treachery of pro-Japanese politicians, declared war on the allies. The Japanese were not such fools as to entrust the Siamese army with any important work, but I believe they did do one or two minor forays in the Shan states. Their military value to the Japanese was nil. Later on we started to organise guerillas in rear of the Japanese, and we did also manage to get some extremely useful intelligence. This was done by Force 136. The guerillas were never allowed to fight, as the war never reached Siam, but they have tremendous ideas as to what they would have done had war broken out. They did practically nothing apart from the some intelligence gathering and the shielding of some allied airmen who had baled out. Yet, on the above record, and taking into account what they *would* have done if only given the chance, the Siamese genuinely believe they played quite an important part in bringing about the defeat of Japan. On the above grounds, and also that "they never wanted to come in against the allies, it was only the corruption of politicians that brought Siam in on the wrong side" they almost regard themselves as having been co-belligerents, and were fearfully hurt at the terms of the peace treaty, which almost seemed to treat them as if they had been enemies!

This attitude is almost incomprehensible to anyone who has never been to Siam, though I would point out it is not confined to Asia as there are Italians who genuinely believe they did something towards winning the 1914-18 war. But when you are dealing with Siamese it is essential to remember that, astonishing though it is, they do believe it, and you will get nowhere with them if you assume - because the idea is so fantastic - that they by inference must be deliberately dishonest.

The Siamese genuinely believe that Siam can, and should, become a great power in South-East Asia once more and - and this is the real tragedy of the thing - will do their best to divert a large part of the country's wealth to that end. They cannot see - their pride will not let them see - that Siam cannot ever hope to be a power in the modern world, and that the happiness of the country would be far better served by disbanding the army except for police and ceremonial purposes and using the money saved for social services. In a country where there is not much money, but a fair amount of raw materials, this would be an enormous gain and the loss of security would be nil, for what is the difference between having no army and having an army incapable of defending the country should the occasion arise? The remarks I have made apply equally to the navy and the air force.

The danger for Siam, therefore, is that the peasantry will have to carry this useless burden all the days of their lives and that it will be a permanent brake on the prosperity and happiness of the people, which should be the prime end of all government. This is particularly unfortunate when one realises how much there is in Young Siam, as one might call it, which is good. Their schools, in which they take a great and absolutely justifiable pride, are miles ahead of any I've seen elsewhere in the east, their roads and railways are reasonably well run, as is their agriculture, and they are making fair strides in their medical services too. Many Siamese government officials, singly, of course, and with strict injunctions to mention no names, have told me that if only the power of the army could be broken, all would be well: but fear of being the first is a great deterrent, and another is the inate politeness of the Siamese. This raises a point of absolutely fundamental importance when dealing with the Siamese. They are probably as polite as any people on earth, and the supreme sin is to be rude. If you are rude to a Siamese you have made him lose face, and nothing will ever make up for that. He will have nothing more to do with you. Once, in the course of my duties, I told the Chief of Police that I had given the Japanese sentries orders to shoot Siamese police on sight if they continued to approach the dumps in the company of bandits. But I said all this with the greatest reluctance, and with profuse apologies, and we were and still are the best of friends - and the Siamese police gave up their tricks. If you are rude you are finished, no matter what else you do. Thereafter, with the ordinary Siamese (not the ultra-nationalist politician or the professional soldier) I believe that the considerations which weigh most heavily are economic ones, and I believe ideological and national considerations come after both of these. The Siamese hated the Japanese because they were rude, and therefore would have hated them whatever else they had done. They disliked some of our Indian troops for that reason also. But the reason they disliked having British troops was that they had to pay for them!

Politeness would make it very awkward for any ordinary Siamese to stand up and say bluntly and unequivocally that such and such a thing was wrong and should go. Siam can have a very happy future. Her land has not been fought over or devastated, she has suffered practically no loss of life or of essential materials. She has plenty to eat and produces in fair abundance food which for many years to come will be worth the earth in the markets of the world. She has probably suffered less than any country in the world as a result of the war - except perhaps the South American republics. She has before her, for the taking, an era of prosperity such as she has probably never known before, if she is only able to break the power of the army in politics, beyond all fear of recovery, and rid herself of the vicious circle which, in present circumstances the power of the army brings with it.

One very important result of the army's connection with politics is that it is almost impossible for a really good general, if one were ever to come along, to rise to the top. He must be a good "party" man first and foremost, and any really good general of independent views would be viewed with the gravest suspicion by the army "political" High Command.

And now, what of the army? The army, navy and air force are all separate in Siam, being united only in the inability of any of them to perform the tasks for which they are supposed to be competent - the defences of the country. The army is, however, much the biggest, and is the service with which I myself came into closest contact. But my remarks apply also to the navy and air force.

I have attempted to explain, above, why the army exists in the strength (numerical) that it does. It now remains to explain how it does it, and what sort of an army results. "How," is fairly easy. By the law of the land, every Siamese youth when he reaches military age must enter one of the services for a period of two years. All boys who have been educated at the better schools must enter the services as officers, via the equivalent of Sandhurst or corresponding academies for the navy and air force, and be an officer for (here I'm not very sure of my memory) five years' minimum, I think, and he can only get out of this by doing the normal two years in the ranks. By this means, they raise an army of I think about 200,000 men.

"What" is really pretty easy too, though to understand what sort of an Army the Siamese turn out, the first thing necessary is to banish from your mind all preconceived ideas. Now an army is the most expensive luxury a country can indulge in. It always has been, and is now more than ever so. Weapons become more and more complicated and expensive, and in addition, as man's ingenuity in devising means of destruction grows, arms become obsolete at an increasingly rapid rate. To keep an army modern these days, you have either got to be able to turn out your own weapons from your own arms factories, or else buy them from abroad. Owing to the expense both of the original purchases and even more to the constant need for replacement by new and better arms, either method is going to involve you in fabulous expense. Siam, being a poor and un-industrialized country, has, of course, no possible hope of being less than 10/15 years behind any - even second rate - power. This poverty has another, and probably even more disastrous effect, and that is that the pay and amenities of the troops are both pretty well non-existent. For instance, a first year recruit is paid per month Ticals 2, 8d at present exchange. Admittedly this is at the present [1946] depreciated rate of exchange. But even at the normal rate before the war it would only have been 3s.8d per month, which also is quite inadequate. A second year recruit gets Tcs.4. They get food, but no amenities to talk of: and they get nothing extra for wives and families. These two classes embrace, of course, the bulk of the Army and the pay of all other ranks is correspondingly inadequate. The results can be imagined. Everybody loathes the Army and takes not the smallest interest in it. They live only for the day when they can get out. The rank and file loathe it most of all, as they see coolies getting anything up to 20 times their pay, and not being ordered about and drilled into line, which the Siamese dislikes almost as much as the

Burman. Nobody who knows anything about human nature in general and the nature of the soldier in particular will be surprised when told that everything movable which can be flogged in the bazaar is flogged in the bazaar, provided even a reasonable hope of getting away with it is offered. Training is also affected, and certainly in my regiment - the one I became attached to in Ubon, there was no training at all, as the colonel couldn't hire coolies for the various duties in the lines for less than 3 ticals a day (from memory), whereas he could use his own men for 2 ticals a month. This, of course, did not assist the young recruit in learning the art of war, and made him even more browned off than he was before.

This is not a very good start for forming a streamlined fighting machine on present day models. But even that isn't the worst. For to understand the Siamese Army, you've got to understand the Siamese soldier. Now you and I have behind us a tradition of, say 1,000 years, in which the army has been regarded as an instrument of defence and, if necessary, of attack, and the greatest dandy, who may spend his peace-time army career between Cowes, Ascot and the London season, none the less realises quite clearly that if war comes, he has got to be prepared to go and fight and, if necessary get killed. And that has so completely become our conception of our army, that we take it as self-evident that others will automatically regard their army in the same light. If you can think that, you will have no chance of understanding the Siamese Army at all: for to the Siamese the army is not an instrument of national defence, but an emblem of national pride. If you don't understand that, you may as well give up the unequal struggle. Siam is, in some ways, a young nation and Siamese want to be able to point to their army and say "See, we, Siam, have also our army." But the Siamese would not associate the army with such unpleasant ideas as death on a battlefield or months spent living in vile conditions in a jungle in the monsoon. You, gentle reader, join the army knowing you may have to fight a war. The Siamese joins the army on the very clear understanding that he is not going to be asked to fight a war in any circumstances whatever, and the Siamese would not stay long when the real war started. And if you feel like that about the army, it makes not a pin of difference how many guns, tanks or aircraft you have. If the human beings that compose an army don't want to fight, the weapons won't fight by themselves.

This may sound hard on the Siamese. I do not wish to be. I like the Siamese very much, and have made many good friends there. They have many fine qualities, but a willingness to indulge in war doesn't happen to be one, and without that you'll never make an army. It isn't that they aren't brave: they'll fight dacoits [bandits] all right - they can see some object in that, but to go donkeys miles away from one's own village and fight a war in which one is not even remotely concerned personally, seems to be the height of folly.

It will be seen that I was ideally suited to help re-equip and retrain the new Siamese Army. Wake up, we have reached Korat.

*   *   *

We got in at about 8 am and went straight to the barracks, which were extremely comfortable. I slept well after a long day in the train. The day afterwards, of course, I first went and paid my respects to the Div Comd. Major Gen. Han. Songgram, a very pleasant fellow, but on the usual model, and his chief of staff, Col. Yisit, a cheerful back-slapping individual, and the most efficient soldier I met in Siam. There were various junior officers too, and everyone was very pleasant. I then went round to the Air Force Club, where I met Hudson, of Force 136, and Holliday, of OSS which is the American equivalent of Force 136. These two had been engaged in arming the guerillas. Holliday had been an American Baptist missionary doctor in Chiengmai, and was a fine type. To have become a special force parachutist after that was indeed a change. We had a party that night - any excuse is good enough for a party in Siam.

At this time I was not very clear what was to be my role: so I thought I might at least start off by finding out the dispositions of the Siamese troops in my area. That evening the general gave a dinner to all of us, including Holliday and Hudson. It was a terrific blow-out, and was followed by speeches similar to those which I had heard in Bangkok.

That day, and the following day also, I made the acquaintance of the Governor of Korat, who was also Governor General of Paksam, one Nai Udom. He was a most remarkable man: extremely capable, very decent and upright and I believe with a real genuine desire to see that Paksam was well-governed. I should say he represented New Siam at its best. I believe he was not entangled in Bangkok-level politics. He put up a very good show in the war, having been of great assistance to us though very carefully watched by the Japanese, and was put up for a British decoration, though whether he got it I don't know. I had lunch and dinner with him, and he was not only good to me personally, but also officially gave me considerable help, chiefly from a distance, as I soon went to Ubon.

Orders soon arrived for me to move to Ubon, which is the terminus of the railway which leads east from Korat, and is the next biggest town in Paksam. I packed up, took my leave of the General, and went to Korat station to wait for the train, and while so doing went and had a look at the various sidings, railway sheds etc. Korat was the only place in Paksam raided by the RAF, and was the furthest place east which they went. What a mess! They sent over Liberators, which came over, with no air or ground opposition in broad daylight at 1500 feet, and in all they dropped 370, 500 or 1000lb. bombs of which over 340 fell in the station area. There was some damage, believe me. However, that had been some months before, and they had long since had two through rails, but had not been able to do much else. It is worth adding here that from Ubon to Bangkok there were no breaks in the line and the line was in good condition. The only bottleneck was rolling stock and locomotives, particularly the latter, as so many had been bombed or strafed during the war, or had become unserviceable due to lack of spares.

The train arrived in due course, and by 3 am we were in Ubon, and by 3.30 am I was in bed in the room in the Siamese regimental mess which I was to occupy for the next five months.

As I was in or based on Ubon for the whole of the rest of my time in Siam, it will be as well, perhaps, to explain what was there when I first arrived.

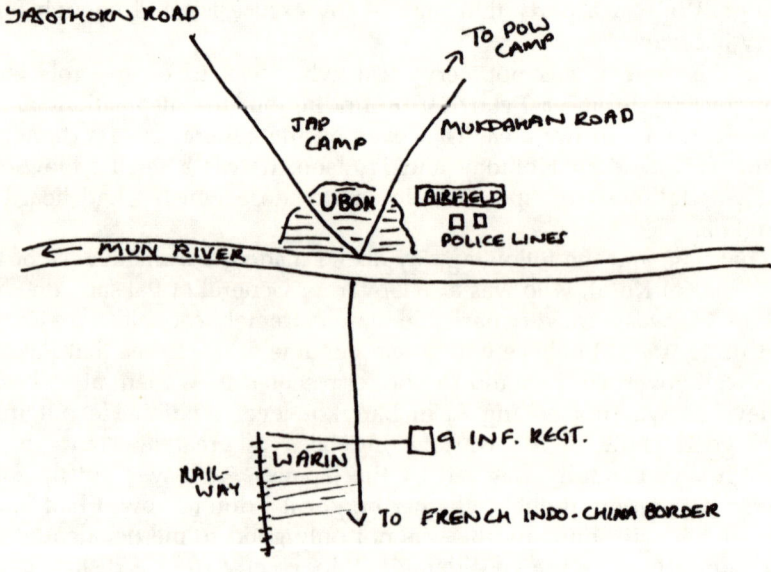

The above plan, not to scale, and only showing essential details, gives a general idea of the layout of the place. Railhead, though called Ubon, was, in fact Warin, and it will be seen the Mun river (pronounced Moon) divided Ubon and Warin. The main Siamese Barracks, in which I was living, were therefore in Warin, and there was about a mile-and-a-half of road from my bungalow to the river. This was about 200 yards wide and was not bridged. On the other side was Ubon with all the government buildings, schools etc. Many of these had been taken over by the Japanese, and there were Japanese units billeted all over the place. There were the police lines, which are shown as they are important because one of the bungalows was the HQ of Force 136, and they were next to the aerodrome which was a first class all weather 1500 yards runway, made of red laterite by our POW's. Needless to say it drained as fast as the rain fell on it. It would take a Dakota easily and would probably have taken a Liberator at a pinch. At Kilo 9 up the Mukdahan road was our POW camp. Regarding personnel, there were 3,000 allied POW's of whom 1200 were UK, 300 Australian and 1500 Dutch. Force 136 was represented by Lt.-Col. Smiley, MC, who had been in the area some time and had come to the surface, of course, as soon as the surrender was signed, and with his HQ of wireless operator, interpreter and one or two others, was established in the police lines. There were two RAPWI officers, Major White and Captain Lang (a doctor), odd extra Force 136 men blew in from time to time, and there was an Australian officer, Major Ewart, to take charge of the Australian personnel. The Siamese had the 9th Infantry Regiment stationed at Warin, and it was to them I was accredited. I should add that I had a Siamese civilian as my wireless operator and we had a B2 set (the same as we had on operation BISON) with which we used to work two skeds every day to Bangkok. The civil were represented by the Governor, Luang Narat Raksa, who lived of course in Ubon, and there were all the ordinary government officials. In addition to them, mention should be made of the Professor. His real name was Nielsen, being the son of a Danish father and a Siamese mother. He had a very charming wife and six very delightful children. He was the government schoolmaster, and the only one of the local inhabitants who could talk English. As such he was invaluable as an interpreter and greatly helped our POWs.

That was the state of affairs when I arrived. The immediate tasks were to get our POWs sent off to Bangkok and to get the Japs concentrated and disarmed. Smiley's and my functions overlapped somewhat, in fact I believe that by the letter of our orders I was doing his job and he mine, but we didn't mind that. We got on very well together and didn't squabble about limits of authority. Roughly speaking, he dealt with our POWs and I dealt with the Japs: we both dealt with the governor when necessary.

There were, as stated, 1200 UK, 300 Australian and 1500 Dutch POWs. Naturally I saw mostly those from the UK, and I have never seen men in finer physical condition. It was a question of the survival of the fittest, and many had died. They had a splendid CO in Lt.-Col.

Toosey, DSO, and their discipline, smartness (in spite of the state of their clothes), general bearing and saluting were as good as any I have ever seen. It was obviously his, and his junior officers' leadership and the discipline of the men that had brought them through not only alive but in such superb physical condition, and I was glad to see Toosey received a well-deserved OBE and that other of his officers also received awards. The authorities were doing everything possible for the POWs and every day there were drops of comforts and medical supplies by Liberators which made the round trip from Calcutta. Not a bad hop. To start off with they tried dropping on the camp, but even with parachutes large numbers of the containers started to let daylight into the bamboo huts, so dropping then took place on the aerodrome, the stuff being taken by Jap lorries and Jap fatigue parties to the POW camp. To cheer the troops up the Liberators usually beat-up the camp, and I remember one in particular who did a sort of aerial bacon-rashering turn. He came over the camp at 50 feet above the trees, and then made four more runs, cutting off ten feet each time. The last run he missed the trees by ten feet at most. Possibly not in the RAF 'book,' but a thrilling sight and we gave him a big hand.

The POWs, not having had a night out since Singapore, poor chaps, were given one night free in Ubon before they left. Six Japanese lorries manned by all the teetotallers the camp could raise paraded the streets of Ubon from dusk onwards and found several 'fares' before the night was done. They certainly deserved a night out after all they had gone through. They were a fine bunch of men. I think perhaps the most remarkable feature was that none of them seemed to bear the Japanese any bitterness, and there was never any suspicion of any POW trying to assault a Japanese. I asked them what they thought of the Japs and their reply was somewhat as follows: "It's all very well to talk of Japanese cruelties to us. By our standards they were cruel, but they were not as cruel to us as they were to their own people." I shall have a lot more to say on this subject when I come to deal with the Japanese, but for the time being let that remark of several who had been through much great suffering and hardship suffice. And another thing that many of them said was that for all the suffering they endured they would not have missed it. I can understand that attitude: to be able to recount experiences few can have gone through, and to have the satisfaction of having overcome such tremendous hardships and difficulties must be a source of pride, and justifiable pride. Another thing which must give a feeling of curious pleasure is to be 'legitimately on the wrong side of the law.' Nobody could have called those men conceited, though after the show they had put up they had every possible reason to be, but one thing they were emphatic about: they were the cleverest thieves living - and I should think they were.

What they didn't hook off the Japs! Bags of nails, hammers, petrol, anything which would raise money from the locals to buy extra food and medical supplies, found its way into the bazaar, though if the Japs found out it meant at the very least a beating up, probably far worse. Dead pigs for extra meat were tied under lorries and driven past the Jap sentries, who only thought to look in, and not under the lorry. They must have developed a fellowship in adversity of a truly deep and wonderful nature, and they looked as if they had. Some of the bravest were the men who kept the wireless which got them news. I think two officers had already been beaten to death when the first one was discovered, but another one soon came into being, concealed in a water bottle which was so designed as to be able to pour a few dregs of water if inspected by the Japanese. A truly wonderful piece of work. But even the Ubon POWs admitted it was only second to that in another camp which was fitted into the head of a broom, with the aerial running up inside the handle.

But enough. These are mere gleanings from the saga of those POWs. They must be allowed to tell their own story in full, which I hope they will. It will be one not only of incredible ingenuity, but also of staunchness, fortitude and self-sacrifice of a very high order in the face of fearful hardships. I am proud to have met those brave men. They left us, after a farewell party given by the Siamese 9th Infantry Regiment, on 25th September. The Dutch were with us a bit longer, and finally left on 25th October.

So much for the POWs. Two or three volunteered to stay on and help Smiley. One was Cpl. Phillips, a Coventry bus driver in peace-time, tough as they go, and with a real sense of humour, which three-and-a-half years of captivity had only served to heighten. He was a first class mechanic, and so was invaluable for Smiley, whose car, which he had taken over from the Jap GOC, a magnificent Cadillac, had the unfortunate defect that it very seldom agreed to start! Then there was Sgt. Thomas, a remarkable man. The son of an English father and a Japanese mother, he had lived a fair length of time in both Japan and England, and spoke absolutely perfect Japanese and English. He had been a travelling salesman for Ford in England, and was a most intelligent man in many ways. So, as can be imagined, his value was above rubies to the POWs. He had nothing much else on: so asked to stay for a bit and was, of course, most welcome and useful.

The normal day, then, was something as follows: I got up and had breakfast (the Siamese were feeding me at the mess bungalow) and then went over to Ubon to the police lines after sending off my morning sked and receiving any messages there might be. The Japanese were at Smiley's house and we gave them any orders there were. Lunch usually with Smiley, and back to take over Jap arms in the afternoon;

wrote my reports in the evening, wrote my messages for the following day, and then bed. There was plenty to do, and lack of a jeep (I got one later) made things no easier, but as I could walk about two mph faster than anyone else in Ubon, I could make up time that way if necessary. Soon after I got there the Mun River flooded, as apparently it does every year, to a width of a mile: and stayed up for three weeks! So morning and evening I had to cover a mile in a sampan, which took 45 minutes, as we had to weave our way through bushes the whole way. But I am digressing. We had better tackle the problem of the Japanese.

My division was the Japanese 22 Ind. Inf. Div. who had landed in Shanghai about the end of 1943, but had gone to Canton some time about the middle of 1944, and then had marched from there to Ubon, taking a year and a quarter to do it, and fighting Chinese all the way. They had originally three regiments, the 85th, 86th and 87th, but had sent the 87th over to Hanoi, I think, and somewhere else in Indochina had dropped their artillery regiment and their Div cavalry. As a result, when they arrived in Siam they only had their Div HQ, 85 and 86 Regts, their Div Engineer unit and Div Hospital. They were, however, greatly strengthened by a large air corps, which brought their total strength to 8919. They were under the command of Lt.-Gen. Hirata and the Div Chief of Staff was Col. Hotta. They were to be my charge for some four or five months, and in that time I had the most wonderful chance of observing the Japanese at close range that anyone could ask for.

First of all, of course, they had to be disarmed. I arranged for a place for the Japanese to dump their arms, which were to be taken over by the Siamese, to be delivered to us on demand. Needless to say, the Japanese were efficiency itself. You went along, were met by the officer in charge plus the Japanese interpreter, there were lists in triplicate, all the arms were laid out in order, where they could be easily counted, the Siamese, Japanese and myself all counted them, ticked them on the list, Japanese fatigue parties loaded them into lorries driven by the Japanese with a Siamese officer on board, and at the far end the Siamese unloaded. Three signatures and all was done. There was a taking over of sorts most days, though things got a bit harder when the river flooded and the Japs had to ferry the arms one mile instead of 200 yards, but they did it all right.

Then the Japanese had to be concentrated. Though most of them were in Ubon there were others as far away as Mukdahan, some 100 miles to the North, and in Ubon itself an area had to be selected. The original idea was the Japs might be going to stay for years: so the area had to have water, and also had to have clearly defined boundaries. Luckily, as shown on the sketch, we had the perfect area, which simply selected itself, and all I had to do was to ask Bangkok's sanction for its use by the Japs and work could start. Actually, it couldn't start at once, as there was a delay over building materials, of which more anon, but the area was agreed on. The Siamese did their best to fight this, as there were five buildings in it which were to have been, and still may be, the beginning of Ubon University, but the area was so good that they had to give it up. However, the Japanese weren't in them long.

From the moment that the area had been selected, my job consisted chiefly of the administration of the Japanese. I have said that there were delays, but really the delays took place in Bangkok rather than Ubon. What was happening was that the Siamese were discovering that there were people in their country who were insisting on things being done in a hurry. This, of course, was utterly contrary to all the traditions of the country, and, of course, threw the Siamese Army Chiefs and Ministers into the wildest confusion. To make matters worse, from the Siamese point of view, there was a good deal of work which had to be done between Siamese Army HQ and the Ministries, and the Army, as a result, found themselves having to chase up Ministries! without the usual time which should always be allowed to elapse - not because it is necessary, but because it is desirable, as helping to preserve that measured and even tempo at which, according to the Siamese way of thinking, life should be lived. The British, of course, knowing nothing of Siam and judging the Siamese by their own standards, couldn't see any reason for these delays (of course, by our standards and values there weren't any reasons) and chased the Siamese even harder, thereby throwing them into even wilder confusion. It was a case of each being right by his own standards.

The way it affected us was that orders were not getting through from Bangkok, and it was not reasonable to expect the Governor of Ubon, who was responsible to the Ministry of the Interior to take orders from me - in fact I had been specifically told I could not give orders to the Siamese until he had had his orders from the Ministry. I hammered away at the Mission to get these orders pushed through, and got a visit from the Brigadier, Nai Udom and a whole lot of hangers on. It was very pleasant to see them, and of course, the usual parties were given but if they had got the orders sent through from Bangkok it would have been all that was required, as I told them. As soon as these orders did arrive, the Governor, and Army, co-operated in every way.

Building materials were the first essential, and the Governor started, through his Nai Amphurs, to buy these up. As they were delivered, so they were checked by the Japanese, the Siamese and myself, taken over by the Japanese, and dumped in their area to start more buildings. The Japanese had been able to get a large amount of building materials by pulling down their scattered camps and re-erecting them in the new camp area. Meanwhile, of course, the scattered Japanese units were pouring in from the districts, being disarmed, and then moving into the new area. The Japanese being the workers they are, it is hardly necessary to add that the camp didn't take long to go up, and once things had started moving, they moved fast. Huge dumps of food were laid in the camp, Bangkok sent up more - which were transported at great labour across the river and to the new camp and three weeks later went back to Bangkok! - and generally the whole camp was getting ordered.

As you can understand, there was a considerable amount of work - and very interesting work - for me to do over this. I had to co-operate with the Governor, the Siamese Army - over the take-over of arms, guarding of the new Jap camp etc. with the Japanese twice daily, with the Siamese police over deserters etc. In fact, while one had no routine, one was more or less the centre of everything, and was dealing every day with different people on different subjects. It was a job of endless variations, in which one had complete scope for initiative and imagination - as interesting a job as one could want.

It would be wearisome to recount the whole history of these months in chronological order: so I shall content myself with touching on various aspects one at a time.

There were the bandits. Anyone who has lived in South East Asia knows what a curse the bandit, or dacoit, can be, and is to the local inhabitants, the government - in fact to everyone. Needless to say, the bandits considered any Jap dump was absolutely fair game, and day after day I received reports at the conference that more stores had been stolen. Now these were guarded by Japanese sentries armed with rifles - they were allowed enough arms to guard dumps - and in any case the stores had been taken over by the Allies: so to condone this sort of thing not only lost allied stores, but also encouraged complete lawlessness; and we kept on saying to the Japs "why didn't you shoot?" Always the answer was that they would next time, but, of course, they didn't. I was getting desperate. I knew, of course, that the reason was that the Japanese, being highly suspicious people, thought this was merely my dodge, and that as soon as a bandit had been shot, the Jap sentry would go up for murder. They were constantly assured they would be backed up and at last the great news arrived one morning "they had bagged a stiff!" Off we all went, Smiley, self, the Japs, the Siamese police and army representatives, the Nai Amphur and anyone else who wanted to come.

There wasn't much doubt as to what had happened. Two Jap sentries had been guarding a petrol dump when they saw two figures some 30 yards up the path - it was a full moon - and went to ask them, with the greatest politeness, though in a language not one word of which they could understand, what they wanted: so far from answering the question in the civil manner in which it was put, one of the figures smote one of the Japanese on the head with a large stick, and it is difficult to resist the conclusion that he had brought it with precisely that object in view. The sentries, we were told, remonstrated verbally, but the locals were clearly in no mood for the niceties of the balanced pros and cons of a peaceful discussion. Harsh words were bandied about, and it was soon clear that there was an imperfect communion of spirit between the two bodies of men. Finally, in despair of bringing the locals to a reasonable frame of mind, one of the sentries discharged his rifle and, though no anatomist, I estimate he hit one of the locals through the liver. This gentleman managed to do 60 yards down the path before "falling out at the side of the road" for the last time. The other, clearly in despair of ever convincing the Japanese of the essential justice of his case, moved off at a good round pace and the jungle swallowed him: Having received this account of "how the accident occurred" we were then privileged to tread the last 60 yards, being clearly marked as from time to time a spot of blood had been ringed by the Japanese with leaves as irrefutable evidence. But the most irrefutable evidence of all came at the 60th yard - to wit the stiff in situ. The case had been clearly reconstructed to everyone's satisfaction, the Japs were acquitted and complimented on the spot, and as a result realised they were not going to be let down, though I'll swear they thought they were going to be!

I then had the unpleasant job of going down to the Governor's office and telling him that one of his flock would, most regrettably, have to be considered as permanently off the electoral roll and would be unable to assist the national exchequer by the payment of any more taxes or by any form of productive work. I expected the long drawn sigh of regret from the father of his people, possibly coupled with some observations about the transience of all things human. Soon after that I saw myself tip-toeing out of the saddened man's office. I needn't have worried. He let forth a shout of delight - not even the inevitable loss of revenue seemed to worry him - and was with difficulty restrained from lining up the office staff and leading them in three deafening cheers. The only part of the expected programme which materialised was the "long-drawn sigh of regret," but that was because we had not got the other bandit as well! It was clearly a case of "how beautiful upon the mountains are the feet of him that bringeth good tidings" - with me cast in the title part!

But joking apart, I can understand - and so, I know, can many of my readers - just why the bandits get no sympathy. They are one of the most unmitigated curses with which South East Asia is afflicted.

This didn't stop the bandits, but it made the Japanese realise they were going to be backed up if they fired, and, though further thefts occurred it kept things reasonably within bounds. The Japs got two more bandits before they left. Things did, however, get a bit more serious when, later, we had our big dump at the railway station and it was reported to me that the bandits were coming in at night and the Siamese police were standing behind them with loaded rifles ready to shoot the Jap sentries if they offered resistance! On this occasion I went to the Chief of Police and told him, with the deepest regret and with profuse apologies, that I'd ordered the Japanese sentries to shoot the Siamese police at sight if they tried it again. I can well remember that short interview. He was on his balcony, at a table, and his office staff inside: the usual rustling of papers, clacking of type-writers and general indications that work was being shelved could be heard: and then I started to talk, and you could "hear" the silence inside that office. After I had finished, the Chief said "I'm so sorry, I know we have many bad men in the Police" and off he went, and that one stopped and the Chief and I remained excellent friends, of course, the Police for years have been the most awful rogues - the rank and file at any rate, and, being underpaid, make it up with rake-off and squeeze.[2] They are in with the bandits everywhere, and it can well be imagined that the public have nothing but fear towards them. It is a pity. In the old days the Police were - I believe - unarmed, and there was a provincial gendarmerie, run and officered by Danes, well-paid, very smart, and not corrupt. They were a very fine force, and kept banditry down to nothing, as the public knew they were not only on the side of law and order, but also were strong enough to protect them. So the public - who always know who and where the bandits are - were not afraid to give them away. Some years ago the Siamese said they would do away with the gendarmerie, as they wanted no foreigners, and arm the police instead. The result has been catastrophic, and it's hard now to see how the union of the police and bandits can be broken. The whole thing has become a vicious spiral, and next to the curse of a politically minded Army, this is probably the greatest curse Siam has to bear. Of course, it is not so bad in some places as it is in others.

We only actually caught a thief, as opposed to bandit, and he was working in the railway yard when the dump was there, in the Jap luncheon hour, and was taking bar copper, of which there was a lot, and burying it under the track with a view, if necessary, to digging it

---

2   The Police, thereafter, contented themselves with firing shots into the Jap camp at night from the road nearby. This was a nightly occurrence, but they never hit anyone. The only time they managed to wound a Jap was when they threw in a grenade. It was never proved it was the police, but I have no doubt it was the Police or their friends.

up months later. One of the Japs saw him from 100 yards away, and caught him. I finally had to go to the Nai Amphur's office, where the statements of the Japanese witnesses (three of them) took four hours to take down! They were each about a paragraph long, but had to be translated into English, and then by me into Siamese, and then the reverse process took place as the Nai Amphur asked every imaginable unnecessary question and the Japs always answered twice off the point before giving the right answer: I didn't like to think what was going to happen when we went into court and had a defending counsel, but luckily the man pleaded guilty and got 18 months! I was sorry for him, but one gets a "case" so seldom that one has to be firm when you do get one. So much for the bandits.

Then there was the visit of the 7/2 Punjab Regiment - not all of them, just a company. All the Japanese arms etc had been collected by early November,[3] and were in the custody of the Siamese. Early in November, therefore, I was summoned down to Bangkok to decide how best to dispose of these arms, and we persuaded the General to have them railed to Bangkok docks, loaded into LCT's, taken out to sea and dumped - a method at once easy, foolproof and final. Soon afterwards, a company arrived up, under Major K. McCutcheon, and it was very pleasant having them for a week. They were fine troops, and it did our name good to have them for a week in Ubon. They finally went away with a complete train load of arms and ammunition, having greatly enjoyed their freedom after the restricted barrack life of Bangkok. I did my best for them and they were most appreciative. The stuff was all loaded onto LCT's and thrown into the sea, and I should have greatly enjoyed going on that trip. It would have been most satisfying not only to have a day or two's sea trip, but also to assist in throwing the weapons of a complete Japanese division where they could do no more harm.

Then there was the question of Japanese rations. "Q" has always been a bogey of mine, but this clearly had to be done. There were two scales of rations, depending on whether the Japs were working or sick, or sedentary, and all scales were worked out in ounces or pounds. There had to be converted into kilograms; then some rations had to issued from Jap dumps, and some purchased locally by the Siamese, and of course there were the usual forms to fill in. However, complicated though it sounded, it worked quite smoothly, as by then I had

---

3   Smiley and all other allied officers and men had left Ubon on 28th October, and I was entirely on my own. The aerodrome, therefore, ceased to be the centre of activities, and all conferences were held in my bungalow.

discovered the secret of getting things running properly - do it yourself for the first two or three times and the Siamese, whether army or civilian, will pick it up quick enough. Throw a whole mass of documents in an alien language to them and expect them to straighten it out, and you'll be in for a whole lot of trouble which you'll have to straighten out yourself in the end in any case: so why not at the beginning?

In some ways the most satisfying thing to do was the bomb disposal. The Japanese had 100 tons of aerial bombs in Ubon, and the obvious thing was to blow them up. Needless to say, it took a good many signals before I could get leave - not because the Mission was slow, but because the decision had to come from - I think - the RAF who couldn't make up their minds if they wanted them or not. However, leave did arrive at last, and we started. I had previously recced a jungle aerodrome as a perfect site. This was not the main aerodrome but a satellite which the Japs had built with our POW labour at K.M. 10 on the Mukdahan road i.e. just opposite the POW camp. This had been almost completed when it dawned on the Japanese that the wishes of the Emperor over winning the war might not be carried out, and they enlisted the co-operation of our POW's to dig a number of trenches across the runway. These, of course were perfect for our purpose. A ton in three of these and we had three good big craters. Thereafter we used to send up six tons at a time - two tons in each hole. The three fuses were lit at the same time, but did not all burn the same speed, so we usually used to get three separate explosions in the space of about half a minute. They shook Ubon, which was six miles away, but we sent up the whole 100 tons without accident. The villagers, of course, had been warned through the Governor. The most remarkable part was that even after 100 tons had gone up, I never discovered one single bomb splinter either in the craters or on the aerodrome.

Then there were my special pets, the machine tools. It had been the intention of the Japanese to have a large air training centre, with workshops, at Pakse. This place, of which I shall have more to say, is 70 miles from Ubon and is in Indo China. To get to it you motor from Warin to the Mekong, 70 miles, and ferry across the river. The Japanese, to build up these workshops, had had a very large number of machine tools sent up to Ubon by rail. From there they had to be sent down the road, and as the end of the war found the operation incomplete, these tools were scattered all over the place, the furthest having reached Mu Ang Kao, the village on the Siamese side of the river opposite Pakse. If possible, I'm even less of an engineer than I am a horseman, but just as even I should think a Derby winner 'looked a good horse' so these machine tools looked pretty good to me. There were lathes, turning machines, compressors and a whole mass of stuff I'd never seen the like of, much of it brand new; and with England starved of machine tools I didn't see why they should be wasted. I asked for some engineers to come up, which they did, and they threw out a few which were useless but the rest they said were worth tens of thousands of pounds. So I told the Japanese to start getting them up to the railway station. Now many of the machines weighed three tons, and could not be taken to bits. The Japanese had no cranes. (They did have one tractor. It had been totally under water for three weeks during the floods, but they scrubbed it out and got it to work. It would only do three mph, however, so it could only be used for unloading at the station.) And their lorries were falling to bits. Also, some of the tools had to cross the river. Yet they got them all to the station!

They loaded them by hand, pushing them up ramps, and with egg-shaped tyres and springs like croquet hoops brought them back in triumph to Ubon. I hope some of those machines were subsequently put to good use in the reconstruction of the various countries which have been devastated.

They are a most curious and remarkable people, and by way of an interlude I will here give my views on one of the war's greatest enigmas, the Japanese soldier. He is a very complex character, the product of so many good and bad characteristics, that he is bound to be hard to understand. I shall, therefore, start off by saying what I think his main characteristics are, and try and draw a picture of him at the end.

He is fanatically brave. Of this I think there can be no doubt whatsoever. If one understands by bravery an indifference to one's own death or suffering, it is only necessary to look at the record of the Japanese soldier in Burma or anywhere else during the war. As General Slim said, "Many soldiers say they will fight to the last man and the last round: the Japanese are the only ones who do." He ought to know.

He is 100% disciplined. It is perhaps worth mentioning here that of the whole force I was in charge of we only had nine deserters, one of whom was caught. Considering they were only 60 miles from the F.I.C. border, and there were Japanese fighting in that country as bandits assisting the Annamites, there was plenty of temptation and opportunity, and it is a tribute to their discipline that more did not try. Curiously, almost all the deserters were from the Air Corps. A 207 BMM friend of mine who was up in Chiengmai said the Japanese Lt.-Gen. there stood no nonsense from his own men over desertion. Everyone who could possibly be in any way responsible was arrested and punished, and arrests usually ended only at the CO of the battalion concerned. The charge against all such people e.g. the platoon and company and battalion commanders concerned was one of being "inappropriate," apparently a very serious charge to judge from results!

Founded on the belief that the Emperor is divine and that to die for him is the highest blessing a man can want, even a lance corporal becomes, to the private, the representative of the Emperor and, therefore, sacrosanct. But, and this is a point on which all POW's I spoke to were absolutely emphatic - the discipline was founded on fear. It is literally true that a major-general in the Japanese Army will go on parade and will, if he feels so inclined, knock a lt.-col. flat on his back on the parade ground, and nobody will think it anything out of the ordinary. But if the lt.-col. hit back, he would practically have struck the Emperor, and I don't like to think what would happen to him. That goes right from the bottom to the top. The first class private bashes the 2nd class private, the superior private the two of them, and so on right up, literally, to the very highest ranks. It is hard for anyone who has not come into contact with the Japanese to realise that, but you'll make nonsense of the Japanese soldier if you don't realise that it is literally true.

They are the hardest workers in the world (I say this even after seeing the Siamese!). Now don't mistake me, I don't say they are the most intelligent; I say they are the hardest workers. They have been used to working with their hands for so long that they automatically know how to work as a team. Give a party of British or Indian Other Ranks a job of say, loading a train, and what happens? The man in charge appoints six men for this, two men for that and so on, and as one job is finished has to put the men concerned onto something else. Not so the Japanese. When they are given a job like that, every man knows just where to go, knows just how a particular load should be lifted, whether it is a one man load or a 20 man load. The standard time, for instance, for loading a Japanese 75mm gun onto a lorry without ramps was 30 seconds! When in Bangkok our people took some figures of the comparative abilities of the various troops. The figures were pretty illuminating. They came to the conclusion that if an average British or Indian troop could lift one ton in a given time, an Indian Sapper and Miner could lift two-and-a-half tons in the same time, and ANY Japanese could lift three-and-a-half tons. They had to be seen to be believed.

They are by nature somewhat cruel. Most people would put this top of the list, but don't forget, gentle reader, that you have, for the last four years, read stories which, though true in essence, have been distorted by propaganda. By our standards they are, but what you must remember is this: as soon as you get Mongolian blood you get a complete indifference to suffering, not only in other people, but also in yourself. As our POW's said: "The Japs may have been cruel to us, but it was nothing to what they did to their own people." They told me of when they were working on the Siam-Burma Railway; Japanese wounded would come down the line, starving, rotting, sometimes with men who had been dead for three days in the filthy cattle trucks they were travelling in. Did the units through which they passed raise a finger to help them? No. In the Japanese Army you will help a man in your own regiment - outside that you'll do nothing to help at all, and nobody would ever expect you to. The POW's told me of one Japanese regiment on the line which refused even to give another regiment water. I ran up against this very early on: "We can't do that sir, it is in the other regiment's area." And I don't believe I ever really broke it down. Furthermore, if cruelty could ever be said to be healthy, the Japanese form of cruelty is a healthier type than the Germans. Say a Jap sees you slacking; so he hits you on the head with a piece of bamboo, and that's that. Don't think I'm saying that that's the right way to treat POW's, but quite apart from the fact that they do that and worse to their own people, on the whole, their cruelty is nothing like as bad as the bestial cruelty of the Chinese (our Allies, so of course we hear nothing about this). There were, of course, exceptions. People like the Kempei Tai, the Secret Police, were pretty bestial, there's no doubt about that. But generally, they are certainly nothing comparable with the loathsome, calculated, sadistic cruelty of the Nazis, who, in my opinion, despite having had hundreds of years of Christian and european civilisation have a record of crime behind them unequalled in history. Nothing the Japanese have done holds a candle to them. What I have written here may come as rather a rude shock, but before you discard it as pure nonsense, reflect on whether you yourself have had any source of information about the Japanese at your disposal other than a press which, particularly in wartime is hysterically prejudiced and capable of any amount of exaggeration. What I have written above comes from the lips of men who had been prisoners of the Japanese for three-and-a-half years, a period which had included work on the Burma-Siam railway.

They are, by our standards, a poor people from a poor country. As the Japanese said, "You call us expansionist, but how do you suggest that 80 million people should live in islands the size of Japan?" Do you know the answer? The result, of course, is that they are terribly poor, and as a result have learnt to use anything to get along somehow, no matter how. And it is that which has made them such amazing improvisers: and it was largely his ability to improvise which made him so dangerous as an enemy in South East Asia. A Japanese transport column is a typical example. The Japanese will take lorries which we would have put on the scrap heap two years and the Americans four years previously, and somehow they will make it go. A Japanese transport column looks the most passed out collection of rubber and scrap iron you would see anywhere, but somehow it gets there. I have always heard it was possible to drive a car with a tyre stuffed with straw - only with the Japanese have I done it.

They are almost totally dishonest. I am under no delusions about whether or how far I could trust a Japanese.

He has a tremendous pride, pride in his race, pride in what he has done, pride in the fact that he certainly did believe he was set apart by fate to rule the world, and, arising from that a sublime belief to do anything he turned his hand to. When I was with the Japanese, they were naturally somewhat bewildered, and their attitude was hard to define, as I think it was produced by two conflicting ideas. On the one hand they felt deep shame that they, the invincible Samurai, who above all things despised men who surrendered in battle, were themselves prisoners. On the other hand they felt that their main armies had not been beaten in the field, that they had only been beaten by a force so diabolical that nobody could have resisted it, and that furthermore they had obeyed the commands of the Emperor, which must always be right. None the less, they were puzzled and badly shaken.

They lack imagination. This showed itself in the war: stereotyped plans, inability to cope with the unusual situation, or to make new plans to meet new needs. So sure were they that they were invincible - and the first year of the war seemed to prove how right they were - that they felt they didn't need imagination. Their bravery, their toughness, and above all their merit - for were they not the sons of Heaven carrying out the Emperor's will, would sweep them to victory, despite all odds.

Those, in my opinion, are the characteristics of the Japanese soldier. It is hard to like him, but few could fail to admire him. I certainly admired him. Tough, brave, disciplined and hardworking, it is improbable that he will ever again be a soldier. If he were, the question would be, "Once the illusion is shattered; once the foundation of his iron discipline and blind obedience is taken away, could he ever build it up on any other foundation?" Assuming he is not going to be a soldier again, the question will be, "Will he be able to apply those qualities, which he has learnt largely in his capacity as a soldier to his civilian life; or will the fearful devastation of Japan, when he gets back, added to his sense of defeat, so demoralise him that he will just chuck up the sponge?"

I believe, myself, that if the Japanese can get a new, and better, vision of the future, and can eradicate some of their worst faults, that their innately great qualities will carry them back to a new, and more healthy recovery. But it will take time.

*   *   *

Early in November, news arrived that all the Japanese were to be moved from Ubon to the Nakon Nayok area, which is some 80 miles north-east of Bangkok. There all the Japanese prisoners were to be concentrated. So all our beautiful camp was wasted! However, I was very pleased, as it got the Japanese one stage nearer Japan (I later heard that nearly all got back there by August 1946) and also relieved my very good friends in Ubon of a heavy burden on their economic resources. I realised that to hand over 150 lorries, the Japanese semi-military stores, the machine tools, and all the rest to the Siamese would merely result in the whole lot being flogged in the bazaar, and so I got leave from Bangkok to keep 500 Japanese for guarding and loading the stores at the station. So the process which now began was to clear the main camp of personnel and stores, everything in fact, the personnel going to Nakon Nayok and the stores to the railway station. This was a big job, and at one time we had 3,000 tons of food at the railway station without counting the stores at all! However, as ever with the Japanese, the job didn't take long, and as we got about one train every three days, it wasn't long before all the Japanese - bar the 500, had gone, and all our stores were concentrated at the railway station. All that was necessary was to wait for trains, and send them off, and it was then that I sent the one signal to which Mission HQ in Bangkok never produced a come back. I should explain that the Mission HQ was composed largely of regular officers - grand fellows as well as very good at their job - and great friends of mine. Needless to say there were the usual jokes about emergency (or wartime) commissioned officers versus regulars, and half the fun was to try and put one over - by signal on HQ! After all, the war was over, and a bit of humour in one's signals, not only made life better fun but increased one's efficiency (if you believe as I do that humour increases efficiency, provided both ends have a sense of humour, I recommend "You do not appear to have grasped the point" as an automatic come-back if you have the slightest doubt as to whether the other bloke understands what you are getting at. It is calculated to make anyone sit up and take notice!). HQ, needless to say, did their best to put one over on me in return, and it was all done with the best good humour. On this occasion I sent a signal explaining that the hard part of my job had been done and that "my job in future could be done by an ECO 2nd lieutenant or a regular officer not below the rank of full colonel!" They never came back on that one.

By this time, however, there were a few other things to do. In the first place, in addition to being 207 BMM representative, I was also made the representative of Force 136 personnel at Mukdahan (Victor Wemyss and Harry Despaigne with Powling as W/T operator) some

100 miles north and on the Mekong, at Nakom Panom, some 80 miles (Kemp and Maynard) north of that, and also at Nongkai (Bobby Hubart), which was also on the Mekong but north-west from Ubon, as the river bends to the west, north of Nakom Panom. These parties were all purely observers to keep Bangkok informed of what was in the wind. A fair amount was in the wind as, though the French were well established in Pakse, there were a whole lot of Annamites and Chinese of doubtful loyalties milling round further north, opposite Mukdahan and Nakom Panom and Nongkai. Many questions arose, the interplay of this and that national group, local politics, our attitude to this or that group, etc. But one of the chief problems was gun-running. There was talk of guns being run across the Mekong from the Siamese side, under the connivance, at least, of the Siamese, there were accusations by the French of the Siamese harbouring dangerous Annamites. This, I believe, was the reason why the French, thoroughly exasperated, finally made a raid into Siam this year [1946]. They did not cross into Siam into the disputed provinces, which are further south, between Ubon and Mekong. Most of the tales of the numbers of arms run were, of course, grossly exaggerated, but, as Ubon was supposed to be the source of supply, I was asked to find out what I could do about it.

Finding out about gun-running in a place like this is always a question of balance of probabilities only. You are unlikely ever to get a definite figure, as most of the people you are dealing with are in it, e.g. the police, and all you can hope to find out is roughly what quantities are moving about. As there never was any question of the British "clearing the place up" - for after all it was not their job - all the management wanted was to know roughly what was going on. The question was how to find out, and the sort of detective game that ensued was rather fun. It was also somewhat illuminating.

I first of all had to discover the sources, and clearly number one probability was the Japanese. I knew how many weapons they had had, because I'd counted every single one myself. I then compared these with the number of Japanese. The numbers were reasonable. So there was no positive evidence to suspect the Japs.

However, when the Siamese had handed over the weapons to the 7/2 Punjab Regt they had been short by 9 rifles, 25 pistols and 40 pairs of binoculars. Pointer number one - the army officers were in on it, augmenting their miserable pay by flogging Japanese arms.

During this time I was having Siamese lessons every morning with the Professor, partly because I wanted to improve my Siamese, and also, of course, because he was my 'agent,' whom I paid. Had the local toughs known he was giving me information, i.e. had I gone to see him every now and then and so given the show away, things might have gone badly for him, but with me having lessons, it was too easy. He got me a lot of useful information.

The first thing he told me was that when the Japs collapsed, they sold British revolvers in the bazaar not with a view to arming the locals, but with a view to raising some cash against the day of captivity; and they sold British pistols, of course, because they couldn't be traced to the Japanese.

Then he told me a few days later he had very little doubt he knew who the gun runner was - a jeweller in Ubon: and several times I knew I'd seen army officers going in there, including several of those I most suspected.

Then he told me there were plenty of places in the bazaar where you could buy, say, two pistols, but nowhere where you could buy 20. He also told me many rifles were being sawn off as being more use for close range banditry, being easier to conceal.

Then I went to the Chief of Staff of my Regiment, Lieutenant Colonel Chantarapa, a very decent fellow and, I believe honest, who told me that normally about a dozen rifles were 'lost' each year from the Regiment.

Then I went to the Governor and asked him who was responsible for the arms which the guerillas had been issued with, and which had not been returned. He said that he had a list of all arms, which were kept by the Nai Amphurs when not being used for ceremonial occasions or the like, and that as far as he knew there were none missing.

And then the police picked up three Siamese Air Force officers with two rifles on the bus up to Mukdahan. Of course, I had the Professor onto it at once, and he told me what I would have betted on, viz that the question was one of "when thieves fall out, honest men come into their own." The SAF officers had, presumably, refused to give the police their "share".

With this evidence, which I gave to Bangkok, it was easy to draw the obvious conclusions - that while there were some pistols and rifles floating around, their number was limited to perhaps at most 50 rifles and 100/200 pistols. That the Army, Police and Air Force were in on it: that the centre of the whole show was the jeweller: that the Japs were not in on it, and that there was no evidence of big stuff moving (Nakom Panom had reported 400 rifles and 25 LMG's in one convoy - pure scare talk). The management were content with this - as I say there was no question of a clean up as it wasn't our job - and it was great fun thinking it out and unobtrusively getting at the information. It is only a small affair, but it may help illustrate the difficulties with which one is faced when you have no real foundations on which to build. When, for instance, you start off by knowing that the people you have to suspect first are the Army and the Police - precisely those you would suspect last in European countries: when you know, moreover, that even if you put the police on a red hot tip, they'd manage to warn the people concerned before searching, as the people concerned would be their friends. Quis custodies custodiet?

Then there were the refugees. Several nuns and their orphanage children, whom Kemp had rescued from the Annamites with considerable bravery from the other side of the Mekong, had to be sent through to Pakse, and to do that they had to pass through Ubon. There was a Roman Catholic school in Ubon, with a little Siamese father, and I went and saw him several times. There was a convent also, and he went and saw the Sisters, who put up the refugees for the night, and the day after I sent them off in Japanese lorries guarded by Japanese soldiers! We also had some ordinary civilian refugees; the drill was the same except that they stayed in the old French Consulate on the way through.

When the Japs had got really settled, which was by the end of November, I started entering into the social and official life of the place somewhat, and by doing so attended some interesting functions. One of the most remarkable of these was the funeral of eight of the guerillas. The Siamese were tremendously proud of what their guerillas would have done, and this was obviously a great occasion, but I was interested to know how these redoubtable warriors had met their untimely end, as I was not aware that there had been any fighting. I found out.

When the Force 136 representatives were in hiding - before the war ended, there were, of course, arms being flown in, and the guerillas were being trained, though they were not given the chance to fight. However, on one occasion a Siamese NCO was training his class in the loading and firing of the Bren gun: so, in order to ensure that his class should see well, he decided to put them all immediately in front of the gun, and so that the demonstration should not lack anything in realism, he decided to use live ammunition.

First he demonstrated the method of filling the magazine.

The class noted and was duly impressed.

Then he demonstrated the method of placing the magazine on the gun.

The class noted and was duly impressed.

Then he demonstrated the method of cocking the gun.

The class noted and was duly impressed.

Then, by the natural sequence of events he pulled the trigger. And, that, as a demonstration of how to fire the Bren LMG was the most successful part of the demonstration. Because the gun went off on automatic, and when the smoke of battle had drifted away, he had mowed down eight members of his class stone dead! Well, over a number of years I've heard a good many Siamese stories, but I think that one is the "primus inter pares."

Well, it was those warriors we were to pay homage to, and a good knock about affair it was too. The eight coffins, each in a small kiosk of its own, were in a line on the grass in front of us, each, of course, decorated with flowers, photographs of the warrior etc. Behind the coffins were drawn up the guerillas, armed with as heterogeneous a collection of arms as ever I've seen - including a bazooka! We, the assembled notables, were drawn up on the other side at a range of about 20 yards, in a marquee. The proletariat, who had turned out "in very great strength" were milling all round the outskirts, determined not to miss a free show.

The proceedings opened with a speech, after which eight of the guerillas came and stood one opposite each of the kiosks, facing us. Each one had three different types of rifles! and most of them had some difficulty in distinguishing the various types of ammunition, or in mastering the intricacies of the mechanism of the weapon concerned. They did fire three volleys (with live ammunition of course) over our heads somehow, but somehow one had the feeling the whole time that "history was about to repeat itself." I noted without much satisfaction that the man immediately opposite to us clearly had a highly imperfect idea of the working of his weapons, and, furthermore, when loading, invariably brought the end of his barrel well down, so that his rifle was pointing at us. As I thought that loading and firing might easily be simultaneous processes with him, I was glad I was in my correct place - behind the Governor! There was, however, one consolation; it was clearly never the intention to give the Bazooka a try-out.

After this the relatives of the deceased went and stood before the kiosks, and the priests went up one at a time and were given new yellow robes. It was then our turn: we went up in a line and were given joss sticks, and each placed one on each kiosk.

The next part of the ceremony was the giving of alms to the poor. The Governor and the local judge ascended into a wooden tower and threw small change into the crowd, which by now had been allowed in to the area. The result was, of course, as intended, that there was a mob of screaming, delighted urchins milling round on the ground to pick up the coins. Dust rose in clouds, the urchins became more wildly excited as more and more coins were thrown down, and were encouraged in this by their parents and friends who roared their encouragement. This apparent lack of reverence for the dead is a feature of Buddhism, in my experience. I remember at Elephant Point, after Ywathitkon had been bombed, walking through the village the day after, and seeing a villager throwing a lot of corrugated iron and broken bits of timber into a bomb crater. I asked him if he knew how many had been killed and he replied somewhat as follows: "Twenty four: a couple of my family

are under that corrugated iron." It wasn't that he wasn't sorry they had
been killed: he was. But once they were dead, there was little sense of
reverence for their dead bodies. He was sorry they had gone, but they
were being re-incarnated. So the earthly robe they had cast off was no
further use to them.

During this time the big guns came into action: a series of
reverberating explosions shook the air: what was happening was that
the guerillas were sending off 1lb slabs of plastic explosive in a small
hole about a foot deep some 50 yards away. At that range they make
quite a good crump!

The actual burning was not to take place that evening. However, as I
was going to bed that night I saw a series of flashes from the direction
of Ubon and heard a number of perfectly terrific explosions, and when
I passed by the following morning all that was left was a line of eight
heaps of ashes.

It had been an interesting ceremony, and not without its humorous
aspects as well.

Another interesting ceremony was the annual constitution day
ceremony. This was held on December 10th, and the official ceremony
took place in the hall of the Governor's office. I have made a small plan
of the building:

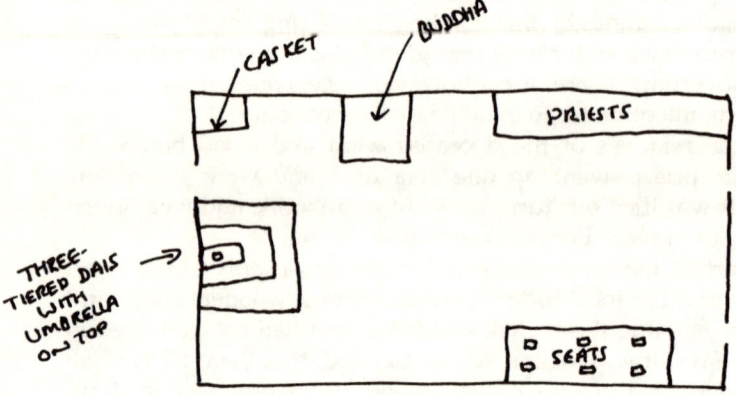

The proceedings opened, after we had taken our seats, with an
orchestra performing outside in the passage. Then in came the priests,
10 in all, and sat cross-legged, facing us on the dais. The Governor then
made his obeisances to the Buddha, after which he took the copy of the

constitution (there is one given to every provincial capital in Slam) and placed it on the top tier under the umbrella: he then took a long piece of string, tied one end to the hand of the image of the Buddha, and passed the string through the hands of the priests.

The priests were then approached by a very old man from amongst the audience, who asked them to say the prayers. This they did, and it really was most impressive. The priests remained absolutely motionless, never for one second let go of the string, and, led by the priest nearest the Buddha, chanted the prayers for three quarters of an hour. The prayers were all in sanskrit, and their unison and timing were absolutely perfect. It was a most unusual and haunting sound, and I can well understand it would give one the impression of being almost transported above the cares and vanities of this world - its object presumably. It almost succeeded in giving me that idea.

After the prayers had been chanted came the feeding of the priests. Meals were brought in and placed before the priests, but could not be eaten until they had been formally proffered by devout Buddhists. This, of course, was performed by members of the audience, who left their chairs formally to offer the food to the priests. We watched the priests eat their meals, during which time the orchestra outside made their presence continually felt in a big way.

The meal finished, the priests offered a short prayer of thanks, the constitution was returned to its casket, which it would not leave for another year, the string was rolled up, the priests filed out, and a most interesting and dignified ceremony was at an end.

There were other ceremonies which the priests attended, and at one of them I had a most charming experience. The chief priest of all Siam was there on that occasion. When the time came for him and the others to go, we all stood up, of course, and as he passed me he just stopped for a moment and asked me how I was. He didn't talk to anyone else on the way out: but I was the stranger in a strange land, and he wished, therefore, to put me at my ease, and let me know I was welcome. Then he passed on. It was a very small act, but it was one of natural, graceful, courtesy, and made a very great impression on me. I can remember the kindly expression on that old man's face as clearly today as then.

There were many other ceremonies while I was there, but the rest were of a far more worldly nature. There were horse races every Saturday anyway, and special events, of course, on every ceremonial occasion. I took to going to these, as I was the representative of the British, and one met everyone there, as the Siamese are almost as inveterate gamblers as the Burmese. They were comic shows: tiny little ponies, ridden bareback by boys aged 10 or 11 years of age, but my word they rode hard. Needless to say, the tote ended up with most of the spare cash in Ubon by the end of the day. The local judge was the president of the turf club, and I used to go up to the members enclosure and drink coffee and tea and chat to the members - it was a very pleasant way of spending the time.

There were also dinner parties and theatres, open air ones. We had a big show at New Year, the turf club giving a dinner and theatre on New Year's eve, and the Governor giving a dinner and theatre on New Year's day. I had sufficiently improved my Siamese by this time to make speeches on these occasions, and they seemed to go down pretty well always. Nobody was prouder than the Professor, particularly first time, as I had not told him I was going to do it, and he suddenly saw and heard his pupil addressing the locals in their native tongue! I must say, I was a bit nervous first time.

The greatest celebrations, however, which consisted of three days and nights' continuous dinners, horse races and theatres, and a really excellent drill and athletic display by the schools, were on the occasion of the signing of the peace treaty. These celebrations took place on January 18th, 19th and 20th 1946. Previous to that, things had been on a somewhat equivocal footing. We had, until then, technically been at war with Siam, and this did put one in a difficult position. You couldn't, legally, help the Siamese in any way whatever, and you couldn't legally attend any official ceremony in an official capacity. The latter point didn't worry me at all, as I could say that I was not really an official, but it was very hard to have to go on telling the Siamese I could not help them over transport when 150 Japanese lorries were lying idle. Between ourselves, methods were discovered which didn't break the letter of the law! It is one thing when you are a large formation dealing with another formation impersonally. It is very much more awkward when you are a single officer being most hospitably treated personally by the people you are dealing with officially. I can honestly say, however, I kept such help as I gave within strict bounds. In Bangkok, of course, the British could not, for instance, watch the march past of the guerillas, when they had a big parade. The Siamese were most hurt about this as, as I have explained, they more or less regarded themselves as co-belligerents!

The only other really interesting side to life in Ubon was that which concerned my relations with the French. One of my jobs as a member of the Mission and even more as the representative of Force 136 was to maintain close contact with the French, and to give them full co-operation. Luckily, I had, in Captain Jean de Gannay who was one of the French officers in Pakse, a very good friend of mine in Force 136, and the British Force 136 officers, Hudson and Blathwaite, had done much to help before and after the Armistice, and as a result there was a good solid foundation of goodwill before I started. Moreover, our interests did not conflict - quite the reverse. I was able to let the French have Jap supplies of rice and salt, from Muang Kao, pieces of electrical machinery from Ubon for getting their electrical plant going, and pretty complete information as to what was going on my side of the border. They, for their part, gave me such information as I wanted, and were also very kind to me personally, always receiving me most hospitably.

Consequently, trips to Pakse were always a pleasure, particularly after I had got my Jeep in mid-November. The distance was just about 70 miles from my bungalow to the near bank, Mung Kao, and it was a mile and a quarter across the Mekong. The road was excellent - you could average 40 mph - and lay largely through jungle, with villages here and there. About half way you crossed what was the old border, and moved into the 'disputed provinces!' It will be remembered that after the frontier war in 1941, the Japanese made an 'award' in favour of the Siamese, and the frontier, therefore, moved forward to the Mekong. The case is still (October 1946) under dispute, and both sides are pretty bitter about it.[4] The French, of course, say it was an award which had to be accepted under duress and therefore is not binding, and are adopting a completely uncompromising attitude over the whole thing. The Siamese say that in any case the French bagged the provinces by force at the end of the last century, and so never was theirs at the best of times. As ever, of course, both sides will not be satisfied whatever happens. I went to some pains to find out what the locals thought about their future (they are, as everyone knows, usually the last people to be consulted on these matters), and to a man they wanted to go back to the French. I asked them why, and they said "Since the Siamese have taken us over, there has been a great increase in dacoity; and since they took over we have constantly been made to do government work for which we have not been paid. When we had to work for the French, we knew how long we would be required, and were paid for what we did." The old, old, story: the average peasant is not concerned primarily - or even at all - with this or that ideology or

---

4   The provinces are economically valuable to French Indo China, as they have an exportable surplus of rice, which, in normal years, balances the deficit of the more populated province of Pakse. Unfortunately, in 1945, on top of the war, there was an almost complete failure of the late rains all over Siam and French Indo China, and it was heartbreaking, in October, to see the paddy shrivelling up and dying. They were certainly expecting serious food shortages in French Indo China about July of this (1946) year, and onward until this year's crop was reaped. The situation was made far worse by the unsettled state of the country, which made it well nigh impossible to move rice from the south, where there is normally a big exportable surplus, to the north.

this or that form of government. Government is no concern of his. What he wants is to be left in peace to till his fields and be given reasonable protection from dacoity and oppression, and his allegiance is to whatever government will give it to him. In the case of these provinces, the racial question comes in too. They are largely inhabited by Laos, the one minority in Siam, and whom the Siamese have alienated by years of neglect - a fine example of how not to treat a minority, and one from which Burma will do well to benefit.

In the last 20 miles or so, the road, though it remains flat and level itself, weaves its way through some jungle covered hills, and when one reaches Muang Kao, hills are visible in all directions. That view will always remain in my memory. Jungle covered hills in all directions, Pakse, neat and tidy, across the water, and in between the mighty Mekong, one-and-a-half miles wide, flowing peacefully past. There was something about that scene which gave me, every time I saw it, a feeling of the everlasting power of nature, and made me feel how puny man is, and how pathetic as well as wicked, are his selfish efforts to destroy the good gifts which God has given him. Here was this river and here were these hills. Hundreds of thousands of years before man was ever thought of that river was flowing through those hills, and hundreds of thousands of years after man by his folly and wickedness has destroyed himself, the Mekong will still be flowing through those hills, even though every trace of man's handiwork has long since vanished. I never tired of that view.

One went over by sampan, which took about 25 minutes, and climbed up the bank at the other side. The French officials and officers lived at the residency, a large comfortable stone building, and if full up, or if it was too late for meals, there was an excellent rest house. Pakse itself is just a French provincial town transported to the Far East, with its neat, comfortable houses, its shady boulevards, its plage - a very good one in the Mekong, and is a very well ordered place. The roads, as everywhere with the French, are first class, and there is a main road which goes right as far as Saigon in the south and as far as Luang Prabang in the north - pretty well the whole length of Indo-China.

Normally I only used to stay the afternoon, have a chat with the Civil and Military authorities, and go back in the evening, but there were occasions I was invited to the annual celebrations at Paksong on the Bolevens plateau. This is an interesting place. It is an isolated table top some 40 miles from Pakse. It is 4,000 feet high, and there is a 60 foot cliff all round it, just below the top, except in one place where a road runs up onto the top by a gentle spur. There is no other way up which does not involve going up a rock face. It is very fertile, unlimited water (it has 200 inches in the monsoon) and the Japanese were going to put a division there to hold out till they were all dead. They could have grown enough food and cattle to feed themselves somehow, and with only the road to get traffic up would have taken some dislodging. However, fortunately they gave up the idea. The main town (large village really) is Paksong, and here every year before Christmas the locals come in for the annual celebrations. Most stupidly I have forgotten the name of the hill tribe concerned. The inhabitants in Pakse province, of course, are largely Laos, and there are a good many Laos in Paksong too. One of the great characters of Paksong is 'the pirate.' He was a French Roman Catholic priest in Siam many long years ago, but blotted his copybook by running away with a Siamese nun by whom he had 15 children. He kept a pub in Paksong, but was not there when I was, as there was, apparently, some small matter which he had to fix up with the constabulary in Saigon.

There had been a fair of sorts in Pakse, but it was not up to much, consisting chiefly of gambling booths, but Paksong was really great fun. We drove up in my Jeep, a very pleasant drive, especially as it was getting cooler all the time, and by the top was quite cold. We had dinner in the French officers' mess. There are two platoons of Laos troops there, under a French sergeant major, and I must say the SM did us very well.

We then went on to the theatre, which was great fun. It was chiefly done by the Laos troops, though there were one or two native dances by women, dressed in their best finery. The general standard, by London West End standards, was not high, but it was good merry stuff, with plenty of cracks at the Chinese, Annamites and French, and, what was most important of all, the performers obviously enjoyed themselves. There were plenty of good laughs, and I gave them a big hand, in which the audience also joined in full measure. That, I thought would be the end of the evening, but no, we were to retire to the headman's house. I know what that meant - 'Zu' as it is known at Kohima at any rate, or rice wine. However, we had a most amusing time. The wine is brewed in huge jars, and first on the programme was a ceremonial dance round it by eight women and girls. I thought they seemed familiar to me, somehow, and then realised they'd been one of the turns in the show. They were all relatives of the headman or his wife and were all living in his house - brave man. The room was dimly lit by rush lights but even in the dim light one could make out a vast concourse of people. Then the drinking started. You all sit round and take one of the long cane tubes which are stuck into the bottom of the jar, and suck: as the level falls, more water is poured in, and so the wine gets weaker and weaker. I sucked as hard as ever I could, but as I had my tongue firmly over the end of the tube, managed to take only a small amount into my system, leaving others to reduce the level! Then, however, the individual tests came, and there's no way out of that. You do it one at a time, and as I was the guest of honour went first and so had the wine at full strength. They fill the jar up full, and you have to take enough for them to be able to pour in a full pint of water. The honour of the Army was upheld, but it was a close thing. The rest of the evening passed, for me, very pleasantly with a Laos Chieftain, with whom I discussed a number of subjects which at the time certainly we found most absorbing, the media being French or Siamese. A good evening.

The day after, we were up bright and early for the ceremony of saluting the flag, and in many ways it was the most interesting of all the ceremonies which I witnessed in these parts. The rough layout is shown on the plan.

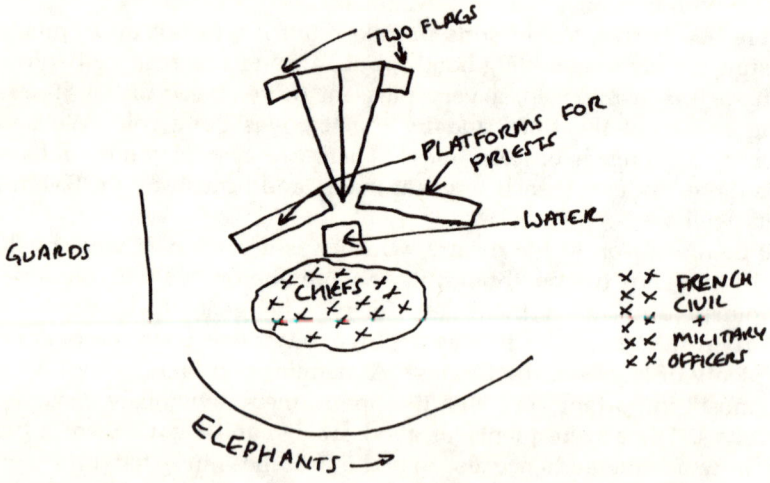

First of all we had the military part of the ceremony. The guard came to the present, and the tricolour of France and the red flag with the white elephant on it, the flag of Laos, were run up side by side. We all saluted, and the elephants were all to bow, the 24 of them. They all did except one, which refused for a long time and then decided to make up for past misdeeds by not only getting down on his haunches but also standing on his head, a feat of balancing at which he made a most valiant attempt and achieved a remarkable degree of success.

After this the Buddhist priests came in and mounted the two platforms - raised some six feet off the ground - on the two sides of the flag mast. They chanted prayers, very similar in type to those I had heard in Ubon, but only lasting some 15 minutes. Then the leading chief got up and recited what was clearly a profession of loyalty, which the chiefs repeated after him, and then three Laos soldiers came forward, one with a rifle and bayonet, one with a spear, and one with what we should call a Dah in Burma, and these were plunged into the bath of water, signifying the watering down of their fury. Then all of the chiefs went forward and drank some of the water, and the ceremony was at an end.

The day was, thereafter, given up to sport; the morning was an ordinary athletic morning, but the afternoon was elephant racing. Needless to say, there was frenzied and hysterical excitement about this, and also a large amount of betting. There were about three or four races, five elephants to a race, straight over 500 yards. Clearly the elephants were the least interested parties to the whole event, and their riders, even with the most frantic efforts never got their charges into more than a fast lope. None the less, we had some close races. I should know. I was judge!

The last event was the archery competition, which I was determined to stay for, as I'd never seen a crossbow fired before. This is a small one, with a bamboo arrow, only used for killing birds, but I was told they do have a large crossbow which it takes two men to load, and with which you can kill a buffalo but only with the aid of a poison arrow. The standard of archery was quite good, but unfortunately I had to leave early, as I was due back in Ubon that evening.

My last visit to Pakse was well, though fortuitously timed, as I was there when the Governor General, Admiral D'Argentlier, paid his first visit to Pakse, and I was in the Residency when he made his speech to the assembled notables. I speak French well enough to understand what he was saying, but Harry Despaigne, who was there with me (also Force 136) is absolutely perfect at French, having been a spy for two years in Occupied France in the war - a fine chap. So there was no question of having misunderstood what he said.

He's a remarkable man. A captain in the French Navy, he gave this up to become a trappist monk, at which he became, and still is, a bishop. De Gaulle pulled him out, and made him an admiral. He is what you would expect. Utterly above corruption, stern and uncompromising, and, like de Gaulle, so obsessed with the greatness of France that he could see neither to the left or the right where France was concerned. In his speech he never once referred to 'the French,' or 'the French Republic' - always 'La France.' The Laos were not thanked for the help they had given to 'the French' but for the help they had given to 'La France.' He made it absolutely clear that, while France was going to help Laos in every way, including making it an autonomous state, yet none the less, Laos was, and always would be, an integral part of France. He said a whole lot more, but I won't weary the reader with it all. What I would like to do is to say briefly what are my views on the situation in Indo-China so far as I could gather it by listening to his speech, by talking to other Frenchmen and by general observation.

French Indo-China is divided roughly into five parts, Cochin China in the south, Cambodia in the south-west, Laos for the central half of the western boundary, Tonkin in the north, and Annam on the east and south-east. The Annamites are in much the same position in French Indo-China as the Burman is in Burma except that the minorities are much bigger. All the others fear the Annamites who, none the less, want to rule the whole country. By the Laos the Annamites are not only feared but also hated, in exactly the same way, but rather more so, than the Siamese are by the Laos in Siam.

Now the French point of view seems to me to be somewhat as follows:

1. There is a tremendous amount of talk these days about self-determination of smaller nations, and many are being given it on principle pure and simple. In many cases they aren't fit to govern themselves, and it will simply mean the little man will be handed over to be exploited by the politician.

2. The person who really matters is the little man, not the vocal politician, therefore, if we can look after him better than he can be looked after by his own people we are going to go on doing it.

3. We do not intend to abandon minorities, who will be exploited and repressed by majorities, e.g. the Annamites.

4. We realise we have adopted a selfish policy in the past. We intend to rectify this in future. We shall do more for the locals, and Frenchmen who go out will have to realise they must help enrich the whole country, not just themselves.

5. We shall give political power to the locals as they are able to take it, not all at once and on an abstract principle.

6. If this is to our benefit as well as the benefit of the locals, that is no affair of any other nation.

This policy fits in with the Laos idea admirably, who otherwise see themselves swallowed up by their hereditary enemies the Annamites, and if the French are genuine in their protestations, and I see no reason why they should not be, it will help the Laos along the road to real self-government, when they are well able to stand by themselves. In the past, there is little doubt the French have not done this, and one of the things I dislike most in the French Indo-China is the almost abject respect of many of the people one meets there. But if the French are genuine, I believe it will be for the best for all concerned.

If you believe that French Indo-China should be one indivisible whole; if you believe it is just a dodge on the part of the French to retain political power and, with it economic benefits for a bit longer; if you believe that self-determination should be given at once, on the grounds that only by experience on their own will peoples learn to stand on their own feet politically; and if you believe the white man has no moral right to remain in the East in any governing capacity whatever, then you will not agree with the French.

If you believe that French Indo-China is not one indivisible whole: if you believe minorities should be protected: if you believe the good of the little man comes before abstract theories of government; above all if you believe in the statesmanship and sincerity of the French, then you will probably agree with the policy they are adopting in Laos.

Time alone will tell.

My time in Ubon was drawing to a close. Most of the stores had gone from the railway station, and all the Force 136 stations in the north were being withdrawn. As I was also about six months overdue for demobilisation, Vic Wemyss and Harry Despaigne were to take over from me, both from Force 136 and what remained of the Mission work. They arrived early in February, and I promptly flew to Bangkok. The reason for this was that there was a debt we had owed to the Siamese some time for salt - it was a Force 136 show - and owing to various exchange and other difficulties, the money could not be produced in spite of several pretty strong signals from me. In the end I got so fighting mad that I descended on Bangkok and went roaring in to the General's office. It took me a week, but I got my money, and returned to Ubon in triumph.

There was now nothing more to do. There were the usual leaving parties, I gave the Governor my binoculars and he gave me a very good Siamese silver cigarette case, and on February 14th I was seen off from Ubon railway station, seated in a Jeep - itself on the last coach of the train. I spent four days in Karat, during which time I said goodbye to my many good friends there, and on February 20th motored by Jeep down to Bangkok. I was intending to stay a week with the Mission, who had long since been in a most delightful house on the river bank, but there was a ship sailing on 22nd and not another for a fortnight: so on February 22nd 1946 I sailed from Bangkok, and my last military assignment had ended.

I left Siam with many regrets. The Siamese had been very good to me, and I had made many good friends there. In a world in which nation after nation is getting swept up in the mad race for power, it was restful and peaceful to live in a country where people are still content with the simple joys of life. A great power Siam can never be, and nothing would be more utterly disastrous to Siam than that she should try and be one. But she can be a happy country - in fact few countries can be better placed to find the path of happiness in the international rivalries and mutual jealousies and hatreds of this modern world. Whether she does so, depends on whether she is wise enough to remain, as she is, a backwater in things international: and whether she is able and courageous enough, in things internal, to set her own house in order: whether, in fact, she is able to smash for ever the loathsome political power of the army, and able to bring peace, happiness, security and prosperity to the peasant. For his happiness is the happiness of Siam.

They were good to me, and I wish them well.

Conclusion

There is little more to tell. I reached England on 15th April 1946, and was due for instant demobilisation. As, however, I had 133 days leave due to me, it was not until 29th August 1946 that I finally reverted to civil life.

I had been in the army for very nearly seven years: most of it on active service, and it is inevitable that after as long a time as that, one should have formed some fairly decided views.

War is the greatest curse of our age; the word which best describes it, in my opinion, is waste: waste of time, money, friends, materials, chances, hopes - waste of everything. You would think, then, that those who take part in it would loathe every moment they were so engaged: and it is a tribute to the incredible ingenuity of the devil that it is not so. In war, many find the thrill, the excitement, and the sense of adventure they have failed to find in peacetime. I did. In danger, many find a wonderful comradeship with their fellow men - of all creeds and colours. I did. In war many people see interesting places they could never have seen but for war. I did. The worst part of war is not the action. The worst things in war, in order, are the long separations from wives and families, and the deadly, soul-destroying, everlasting training, after which action becomes a pleasant and adventurous change. Yet that 'pleasant and adventurous change' will be for the purpose of destroying as many of one's fellow creatures as possible at the smallest cost in lives to ourselves - what a fearful thought! I devoutly trust, therefore, that peace, as it can and as it should, will give to all soldiers who, like myself, are returning to civil life, the chances for adventure, comradeship and interest which we found in war, so that the great qualities of leadership, bravery, self-sacrifice and a host of others, which war brought forth, may be in future used for the rebuilding of the world and not for the waste and misery of war.

Bibliography

Suggested further reading which complements John Hedley's memoirs.

Carew, Tim, *The Longest Retreat: The Burma Campaign 1942*. Hamish Hamilton. 1969.

Masters, John, *The Road Past Mandalay: A Personal Narrative*. Michael Joseph. 1961.

O'Brien, Terence, *The Moonlight War: The Story of Clandestine Operations in South-East Asia, 1944-45*. Collins. 1987.

Rhodes James, Richard, *Chindit*. John Murray. 1980.

Slim, FM Sir William, *Defeat into Victory*. Cassell. 1956.

Woodburn-Kirby, S., *The War Against Japan*. 5 Vols. (British Official History). HMSO. 1957-1969

Index